THE FATHER LEADER

BY
PHIL STERN

THE FATHER LEADER

Published by:

Converging Zone Press

P.O. Box 2825

Peoria, Arizona 85380

ISBN 978-0-9828938-2-1

Printed in the United States of America

TABLE OF CONTENTS

DEDICATION

I would like to dedicate this book to three fathers that have influenced me. First, my own father, Paul Stern. He demonstrated to me what it meant to put God first in my life. He laid the foundations of Christ in my life as well as the essential basics of life. He and my mom set a wonderful example of being sold out to the plan and only the plan God has for each and every life. Thank you dad for being that awesome man of God for me.

The second father I would like to honor is Moses Vegh. Moses has been a spiritual father for me. His prayers and support over the years have been without expecting anything in return. At some of the most difficult times, Moses would call me and encourage me. Thank you for your devotion to my life and ministry.

The third father I would like to mention is Tom Pollard, my father-in-law. Tom has been an incredible support to me and my family. His devotion and connection to my children has demonstrated to me the heart of a father. Thank you, Tom.

And of course, our Heavenly Father. Without Him, we would all be lost. Thank you Father, you're the perfect love for us. We are all here because of you!

PREFACE

Where are the fathers today? What an interesting question! Why would someone ask such a question when we see fathers everywhere? After all, we have many children and we have many mothers, so there must be many fathers because these children have to be coming from somewhere. True, we have population and in some countries we have a lot of it, however, population, children and mothers just means we have procreation. My question is where are the fathers, not where did the children come from. Most any male can procreate, but how many males today are truly being fathers and fathering? We can have many males leading, but how many of those leaders in and out of the church are truly "fathering"? That's why Paul stated to the Corinthian church: *"There are a lot of people around who can't wait to tell you what you've done wrong, but there aren't many fathers willing to take the time and effort to help you grow up. It was as Jesus helped me proclaim God's Message to you that I became your father"* (1 Cor. 4:15 The Message Bible).

Think of it as a process of helping your children grow up. There are so many fathers absent from homes that have relied on moms to grow up their children while they are so consumed with making a living. There are so many leaders in the workplace that are so busy growing a company that they have left the position of helping the people around them grow and become better leaders and employees. And in the church we have seen more focus on Leadership, teaching and building one's own ministry, but when it comes to being a father and a voice of a father, I come back to the title question: WHERE IS THE FATHER LEADER? We have become a fatherless society. We are fatherless because of abandonment. We are fatherless because of absenteeism. We are fatherless because of distraction, and we are fatherless because of abuse.

My heart for this book is to bring not only an awareness to the mission we have in bringing the father leaders back to their role and position but to also challenge the men in the body of Christ to step up to the rightful place God has called them to, not only in the home but in the church and in the marketplace. If there was ever a day when the cry the apostle Paul had is more relevant, I believe today is the day. Though we can find ten thousand teachers, leaders, instructors, managers and pastors, why is it so hard to find the true fathers with hearts to lead. Where are the father hearted pastors? Where are the father hearted leaders who can lead with conviction and true authority? And where are the leaders of homes who are not afraid to step up to the plate and be what God has called them to be?

I pray you will be challenged and stirred at the same time. My good father friend and leader Moses Vegh says *"Men are looking for better methods, God looks for better men. Men are God's methods."* Be blessed as you read this book and together let's believe for a rise in the population of true fathers.

CHAPTER 1

THE CRY FOR FATHERS

There is more than a cry for fathers today, there an ear piercing scream, will the fathers step up and take their place! What a tragedy it is to see children raised in a culture with the absence of a father. When you read accounts of men that tell stories about their dad and the impact their fathers had on their life, your heart aches for those children growing up without a father or at least a father's influence. Look what these sons have said about how their fathers have influenced them:

- *My father explained the workings of the world to me. He showed me the stars. Through him I learned to recognize the Milky Way. He explained that it was a blessing to be able to see it on account of the blackout rules at the end of the war. He taught me how to play chess. My mother told me that I should act like a man and always had many things for me to do that were a man's duty,* ***but my father taught me how to be a man!***

- *My father taught me what it means to be honest and true. He also gave me hope and the feeling of security, when he told of how the things that the war had destroyed and left in ruins had been meant to work, but told me at the same time that they would work that way again, perhaps even better than before. He was a true patriarch, not an oppressor—a servant to his family, perhaps its head, provider and steward, but not its master.*

- *From the time he became a man until his death, my father was a servant of God, his country, and of his family. He is my hero because, although he had to suffer much in his life and even though he had to try and survive impossible odds, he never lost his courage and his honesty, even though he often must have felt extremely frustrated.*

- *We were poor, but our house was filled with love and laughter, thanks to my dad.*

The countless stories told about the role men have played in the lives of their children, and yes there are horrible stories as well, but the cry is loud today for the real dads to step up. God created us to need a father's influence and society is bringing us the statistics to prove just how much fathers bring to the life of a child.

The cry is not only heard for the natural children, but the cry is loud in the church as well. Most of this book will tackle the problems and the need for fathers in the body of Christ and who we can bring the issue to in order to see real spiritual fathers stand up. We need leaders, but what we really need are Father Leaders today.

The decline of fatherhood is one of the most unexpected and extraordinary social trends of our time. We see how the need in natural families has been affected and because there is a shortage of Fathers in the church as well, it has affected the body of Christ.

In just three decades—1960 to 1990—the number of children living apart from their biological fathers nearly doubled. By the turn of the century almost 50 percent of North American children were going to sleep each evening without being able to say good night to their dads.[1]

There was a time in the past when not having a father was far more common than it is today, but death was to blame – not divorce, desertion or out-of-wedlock births.[2]Most of today's children who have a father have dads who are perfectly capable of shouldering the responsibilities of fatherhood. Who would have ever thought that so many of them would choose to relinquish those responsibilities?

It has been said so many times and in so many reports that it is decidedly worse for a child to lose a father through divorce, absenteeism or out-of-wedlock than through death. The children of divorced and never-married mothers are less successful by almost every measure than the children of widowed mothers.

Predictions were being made in the early nineties that "Out-of-wedlock births" may surpass divorce as a cause of not having a father in the early 2000s. They accounted for 32 percent of all U.S. births in 1995; by the year 2000 they may account for 40 percent of the total. And there is reason to believe that having an unmarried father is even worse for a child than having a divorced father.[3]

Men are not biologically attuned to being committed fathers. Left culturally unregulated with no accountability in their life and even more, without a spiritual awakening, men's sexual behavior can be promiscuous, their paternity casual, their commitment to families weak. In recognition of this, cultures have used sanctions to bind men to their children, and of course the institution of marriage has been culture's chief vehicle.

Our experience in the late twentieth century society shows what happens when such a sanction breaks down. The decline of fatherhood is a major force behind many of the most disturbing problems that plague us. In the mid-1950s, only 27 percent of

American girls had sexual intercourse by the age of eighteen; in 1988, it was 56 percent, including a tenth of fifteen-year-olds. Fatherlessness is a contributing factor. Teen suicide has nearly tripled in the United States. Alcohol and drug abuse among teen-agers continues at a very high rate. Scholastic Assessment Test scores declined seventy-five points between 1960 and 1990. The absence of fathers seems to be one of the biggest causes of these alarming trends. [4]

In the world view of the family, few people doubt the fundamental importance of mothers, but what do fathers do? World view again makes statements like – much of what they contribute is simply the result of being a second adult in the home. Bringing up children is demanding, stressful and exhausting. Two adults can support and help each other. They can offset each other's deficiencies and build on each other's strengths. While that is true, we know through the Scriptures that fathers bring so many unique qualities to the home. Some are familiar: the father as a protector, for example, and role model. Teenage boys without fathers are notoriously prone to trouble because Dad is meant to be the main source of guidance in their life.

The pathway to adulthood for daughters is somewhat easier, but they must still learn from their fathers, in ways they cannot from their mothers, how to relate to men. They learn from their fathers about heterosexual trust, intimacy and differences. They learn to appreciate their own femininity from the one male who is most special in their lives. But most importantly, through loving and being loved by their fathers, they learn that they are love-worthy.

Current research gives much deeper, and more surprising, insights into the father's role in child rearing. One significant overlooked dimension of fathering is how he plays with his children. From their children's birth through adolescence, fathers tend to emphasize play more than caretaking. The father's style of play is likely to be both physically stimulating and exciting. With older children it involves more team work, requiring competitive testing of physical and mental skills. It frequently resembles a teaching relationship: Come on, let me show you how.

The way fathers play with their children affects everything from the management of emotions to intelligence and academic achievement. It is particularly important in promoting self-control. According to one expert, "children who roughhouse with their fathers quickly learn that biting, kicking and other forms of physical violence are not acceptable." They learn when to "shut it down."At play and in other realms, fathers tend to stress competition, challenge, initiative, risk taking and independence. Mothers, as caretakers, stress emotional security and personal safety. On the playground, as a father, I will try to get the child to swing ever higher, while my wife as their mother would be cautious, worrying about an accident and how dangerous that might be.

We know, too, that fathers' involvement seems to be linked to improved verbal and problem-solving skills and higher academic achievement. Several studies found that the presence of the father is one of the determinants of girls' proficiency in mathematics. And one pioneering study showed that along with paternal strictness, the amount of time fathers spent reading with them was a strong predictor of their daughters' verbal ability.

For sons, the results have been equally striking. Studies uncovered a strong relationship between fathers' involvement and the mathematical abilities of their sons. Other studies found a relationship between paternal nurturing and boys' verbal intelligence.

How much of these statistics are really true no one will ever fully know, but one thing all these stats lead us to believe is the positive affect a father has on his children when he is involved in their lives. This is why we need fathers in the lives of children.

If this is true for natural children, think of what it looks like for spiritual fathers. We have not even begun to touch on the authority issues in our society (we will address that in the next chapter) but we know that when there is an absence of authority in the home, there are real issues to be dealt with. When there is an absence of authority in the church, it causes a landslide of issues which makes home become dysfunctional. We need father and mother driven churches today.

A father driven model is dysfunctional and a mother driven model is dysfunctional but when you put them together the way God intended it to be, we have harmony both naturally and spiritually.

CHAPTER 2

SOCIETY HAS CHANGED THE ROLE OF FATHERS

The rate of fatherlessness has increased dramatically in our culture in recent years. The United States is now the world leader in fatherless families. Here are some of the sobering statistics regarding the impact of fatherlessness on children:

- Children from fatherless homes are five times more likely to be poor, and ten times more likely to be extremely poor.

- Seventy percent of juveniles in reform school and long-term prison inmates come from fatherless homes.

- Children from fatherless homes are twice as likely to be high school drop outs.

- Fatherless children have more emotional and behavioral problems.

- Girls from fatherless homes are three times as likely to be unwed teenage mothers. Adolescents in mother-only families are more likely to be sexually active, and daughters are more likely to become single-parent mothers.

- Boys from fatherless homes have a higher incidence of unemployment, incarceration, and noninvolvement with their own children.

- Ninety percent of all homeless and runaway children are from fatherless homes.

- Seventy-one percent of all high school dropouts come from fatherless homes.

- Seventy-five percent of all adolescent patients in chemical abuse centers come from fatherless homes.

- Eighty percent of rapists come from fatherless homes. [5]

"It's clear that we can positively impact our culture in a number of significant areas if we can make even a small difference in the rate of fatherlessness." – Stats from Rick Johnson[6]

I realize we are not talking about all fathers but, we now live in a society where fatherless children are on the rise. Just look around, we can see a large number of young men who have fathered children yet are nowhere to be seen. The woman takes care of the kids and the father is nowhere near, and when we live in a society where policy and the media exploit this as normal, we will see the numbers continue to rise. I mean, look at the media and see how stupid men are made out to be. I laughed and cried at the movie *Mrs. Doubtfire*. Men are made to look rather silly in a lot of cases. When we have a society which accepts that as the norm and doesn't require men to take responsibility for their children, it doesn't help men strive to be better.

I think we can all agree that public perception of fathers is at an all time low. Why can't fathers be more like mothers? Isn't that what they are always asking? Look at books and television. There are deliberate attempts to downplay fatherhood as a serious and necessary business. The homosexual agenda is pushing stronger every year.

We know the term "New Fathers" or "New Dads" has become popular. Now what is a "New Dad"? The old father was Robert Young in *Father Knows Best*. There was Ward Cleaver in *Leave it to Beaver*. Did any of you watch those shows? I used to. I was young then but when I had the chance, I would watch *Superman* and then *Leave it to Beaver.* I thought Ward was great. He was a great father to Beaver and Wally. He was an understanding, loving, caring male, and so was Robert Young in *Father Knows Best.* They didn't lock their wives in a closet and they were always home on time with their ties still tied neatly and briefcase in hand. I distinctly remember how they always walked in with a smile on their face and would kiss their wife and pat the children on their heads. That father in today's eyes is boring and uneventful.

But, what was so wrong with the old father? I changed diapers as did my dad. He fed us bottles, he took us swimming and of course he took us to church. He did all kinds of things with us. We washed cars and I learned how to change the oil in my car. What about these horrible old dads? I thought they were a good bunch. Nobody had to tell my dad to do those things, he just did it because he was there with me and involved in my life. Today there is almost a demonizing of the old fathers. It goes even further than that as we are told that fathers are sordid, arbitrary and dangerous. That's the new script we have for our fatherless society. My father was not sordid and was not arbitrary and not dangerous! Oh, there were a few times I knew he might be dangerous if I didn't straighten up. He might say "NO" out of love for his children and for the betterment of their life (and his) but this was all considered to be normal parenting or "Father involvement in the home"! His heart was to protect us from those evil men outside or from that bully down the road, and, by the way, we would respond to that treatment, because we loved that man called Dad and knew how important he was. But that dad, the old dad, is demonized in today's society.

It's too bad there are so many children now in America and all developed nations, who can't experience the warmth, care and love of their fathers. It's too bad that there are now so many children (over 50 percent of those growing up right now in the USA) who can't tell their fathers that they love them and who'll never know what it is like to be hugged by their fathers. Even though many fathers pay *child support* to make up for their absence, money is a terribly poor substitute for real love and a real presence in the lives of their children.

Ostensibly, women have been liberated through the efforts of the feminists, and in the process our children acquired a terrible loss. Women's liberation did nothing for men, other than hold them to the duty of remaining the ready and willing servants of women, without men's former right to be compensated for their efforts in being so willingly indentured to women. Not all that long ago the odds of a marriage failing were one in seventeen. That was an acceptable risk. Now, both in the church and out, the odds have increased to one out of every two! That risk is much too high![7]

The percentage of births to unmarried women has steadily increased in the past few decades, from 5.3 percent in 1960 to 36.8 percent in 2005. In 2004, the most recent year for which data is available by all ages, over a quarter of births to women ages twenty-five to twenty-nine (27.8 percent) and over half of births to women ages twenty to twenty-four (54.8 percent) were to unmarried women.[8]

Importance of these numbers is, women who give birth outside of marriage tend to be more disadvantaged than their married counterparts, both before and after having a non-marital birth. Unmarried mothers generally have lower incomes, lower education levels, and greater dependence on welfare assistance than do married mothers. Economic disadvantage may even extend into old age, with women who are single mothers for a period of at least ten years during their life at greater risk of being poor at ages 65 through 75.2 In addition, women who have a non-marital birth have reduced marriage prospects when compared with single women without children. Children born to unmarried mothers are more likely to grow up in a single-parent household, experience instability in living arrangements, live in poverty, and have social and/or emotional problems. As these children reach adolescence, they are more likely to have low educational attainment, engage in sex at younger ages, and have a premarital birth. As young adults, children born outside of marriage are more likely to be idle (neither in school nor employed), have lower occupational status and income, and have more troubled marriages and divorces than those born to married parents.

Today's trends: The percentage of births to unmarried women has increased dramatically in recent decades, from 5.3 percent in 1960 to 32.2 percent in 1995. This percentage was relatively stable for several years in the mid-1990s, but has risen slightly each year since 1997, reaching 36.8 percent in 2005 (preliminary estimate). Data for 2004, the most recent year for which data by all ages is available, also indicate an increase in the proportion of births that occur to unmarried women among all age groups, including women older than twenty. The long-term trend toward non-marital births may be attributed, in part, to an increase in cohabiting unions and births within such relationships. By the mid-1990s, approximately 40 percent of non-marital births occurred to women in cohabiting unions, compared with 29 percent in the early 1980s.[9]

Ten more recent estimates indicate that 49 percent of our

society has also determined there are the fathers who are absent not by choice. These situations are linked to ex-wives' lack of support of paternal contact and letting a fathers' feelings be influential and valued as one of the main streams into their children's lives. Fathers stating this reason spoke of their overwhelming sense of loss and depression, the pain of seeing their children only intermittently, and the fact that an avuncular "visiting" relationship in no sense resembled "real fatherhood" and was perhaps harmful for the children as well. Fathers' own decisions to cease contact were inextricably linked to their inability to adapt to the constraints of the "visiting" relationship. Listen to the heartbreak of this father:

> *"The most difficult thing is not seeing them and not actually being there to see them grow up. If you don't see them for three months or six months or whatever, you've missed six months of their life. You've missed the wee things like, 'Dad, the ice-cream van's here' or 'Dad, I've got homework to do' or this and that. And then you've got to say goodbye to them, and it's very frustrating. And you wonder - I still don't really know what's best - I wonder if maybe it would be better to leave them alone and let them live their life, and it's not knowing what to do, not knowing which is best for them. The feeling you get inside yourself every time you go away: 'Am I doing the right thing by seeing them, would they be better off if I just didn't see them?'... It's basically just a hurtful relationship. There are a lot of men who really care about their kids, but walk away from them, because there's too much hurt on both sides. But a lot of people don't realize that. I used to be one of them, by the way, who thought really badly about a father who hadn't seen his kids in years. People seemingly label these fathers as uncaring people, but sometimes I wonder if in fact they're more caring, because of the hurt involved, and the separation*

- and each time you've got your child and your child has to go back - is really hard, is really difficult. And until you go through it, you can't understand it. And I think especially with younger kids, the quicker a parent doesn't see their kids then their kids aren't really realizing that their dad's not there. Maybe it's less hurtful because both the child and parent have to say goodbye to each other, and both of you are practically in tears. There's a sort of silence between you – it's like continual hurt. And men that don't actually go and see their kids again, I quite admire, because they're minimizing the pain on that child - because otherwise it's continual pain. But the pain never goes away for the father, no matter what he does." (A heartbroken father from England.)

Most disengaged fathers presented a complex combination of reasons for the loss of contact with their children after divorce, rather than one clear cause. Most frequently mentioned (by thirty-six of the forty disengaged fathers) were difficulties related to access, whereas many of the contact fathers stressed the importance of the support and encouragement of their ex-wives in their maintenance of contact and development of a new parental role. Those fathers who received little or no confirmation of their roles as "fathers" by their former spouses appear most likely to become disengaged from their children's lives:

Another heartbroken father says this:

"Definitions of fathering vary tremendously but I personally would equate it with parenting: a complete commitment to one's child, the major responsibility in one's life, a combination of nurturing, encouraging autonomy and initiative within prescribed limits. It's setting the stage to allow a child to grow and develop his potential to the maximum.

"It's a way of living - getting up with your children, eating with them, doing work together, reading with them, hugging them, putting them to sleep, dealing with their fears, and enjoying their pleasures - living with them."

Researchers at Harvard University reached an amazing conclusion: Of those they examined, the most important childhood factor in developing empathy was paternal involvement in child care.

"It is not clear why fathers are so important in instilling this quality. Perhaps merely by being with their children they provide a model for compassion. Perhaps it has to do with their style of play or mode of reasoning. Whatever the cause, it is hard to think of a more important contribution that fathers can make to their children.

The benefits of active fatherhood do not all flow to the child. Child rearing encourages men to develop those habits of character - including prudence, cooperativeness, honesty, trust and self-sacrifice - that can lead to achievement as an economic provider. Having children typically impresses on men the importance of setting a good example. Who has not heard at least one man say that he gave up an irresponsible way of life when he married and had children?"

You would think there might be one positive thing about fatherlessness. Without a man around the house, the incidence of child abuse might be expected to drop. Yet, the rate of fatherless children has skyrocketed as well as reports of child neglect and abuse since the mid 1970s. One of the greatest risk factors in child abuse that investigations found, is family disruption, especially living in a female-headed, single-parent household.

Why does living in a *fatherless household* pose such hazards for children? Explanations include poverty and the fact that children receive less supervision and protection from men their mothers bring home. Children are also more emotionally deprived, which leaves them "*vulnerable to sexual abusers, who commonly entrap them by offering affection, attention and friendship,*" wrote David Finkelhor, an expert on child abuse.

Another group that has suffered in the new society of *fatherlessness* is, of course, women. In this new era concept that a woman without a man is like a fish without a bicycle no longer seems quite so funny. There is no doubt that many women get along very well without men in their lives, and that having the wrong men in their lives can be disastrous. But just as it seems to play a role in assaults on children, fatherlessness appears to be a factor in generating more violence against women. Partly this is a matter of arithmetic. As the number of unattached males in the population goes up, so does the incidence of violence towards women.

Father-absence promotes anti-social behavior as well as criminal activity and psychological problems. Look at these alarming facts:

Delinquency of children, and in particular boys, is promoted by father-absence. The problems with not having fathers in children's lives can be so bad that they can cause an 86 percent increase in the likelihood that a child will become a psychotic delinquent.

Some of the widely recognized statistics of the result of the absent father and the cost our society is paying is alarming. Look at the numbers that are linked to absent fathers:

- 90 percent of all homeless and runaway children

- 70 percent of juveniles in state-operated institutions

- 75 percent of all adolescent patients in chemical abuse centers

- 85 percent of prison youths

- 80 percent of rapists, motivated by displaced anger

- There is also a threefold increase in the likelihood that a child will be involved in gang activity.

- 200 percent increase in the likelihood that a child will require psychological treatment.

- 85 percent of all father-absent children exhibiting behavioral disorders. This is a crucial point for consideration for every attorney, and every judge that separates a fit father from his children. They are PROMOTING behavioral disorders.

- Low self-esteem is suffered by both girls and boys.

- 200 percent increase in attempted or successful teen suicides.

- 63 percent of all successful youth suicides from fatherless homes.

- Academic performance is severely affected.[10]

> *Father-absence creates a significant decrease in school performance, a significant increase in disruptive school*

behavior, a significant decrease in per-
formance on aptitude tests, in cognitive
skills, in terms of grades, and is cumula-
tive in nature; and predicts truancy and
grade repetition. Fatherless children also
account for 71 percent of all high school
dropouts. Some of the affects of this low
academic achievement can be seen in the
substantial increase in men's odds of end-
ing up in the lowest occupations repeat-
ing the "illegitimacy cycle," and ending
up "dead-broke" unable to support their
children.

In contrast to this academic destruc-
tion of children, children with fathers in
their lives "are more likely to get mostly
A's, to enjoy school, and to participate in
extracurricular activities if their nonresi-
dent fathers are involved in their schools
than if they are not." [11]

These numbers are too high and if we don't see a reversal,
they will only climb higher. As was stated in the movie *Apollo
13*, just after the explosion took place on board their spacecraft
–"Houston, we have a problem"! It was also stated by a great
leader in Huston during the course of the crisis, "I believe this
can be our greatest hour." Well, I believe it is an hour for the
church to shine. I believe this is the time when we will see the
real fathers stand up and take their place. I believe that if every
man in the church today will hear the call and do what is required of them, we will and can see society change. It's in our
lap and it certainly is our call.

*"... I'm sending Elijah the prophet to clear the way
for the Big Day of GOD –the decisive Judgment Day!*

He will convince parents to look after their children and children to look up to their parents. If they refuse, I'll come and put the land under a curse. "Malachi 4:5-6 (MSG)

CHAPTER 3

WHY FATHERS? WHY FAMILIES?

Some people say the family is obsolete and irrelevant. It's widely believed that we should forget the whole of family, that the structure of family is no longer valuable to our society anymore because it's the "Old Fashioned" approach to life as we know it. But the roots of family are not something we came up with and it is not finished. True, it's fragile and needs to be strengthened and re-taught to this generation. Why is the family important? The right answer comes from Genesis 2:18, "The Lord God said, 'It is not good for man to be alone. I will make him a helper suitable for him. For this reason a man will leave his father and mother and be united to his wife." Therefore, the family is God's idea! Whether you're married or not, it's not good for you to be alone. You were made for relationships.

Understanding the "Father Leader" means understanding the purpose of the family. I believe the highest leadership role you can walk in is that of a father or mother. So understanding how the whole family works and its purpose is very important.

The usual tactic of an army is to attack and wipe out the most serious threat. I believe the family is the most serious threat to Satan and his mission in the earth today. So many people will sacrifice this precious thing called the family for position, fame and fortune. Open your eyes and heart to see the value of family as I share with you the four basic purposes God intends for your family.

Number 1: The Family Is A Shelter From Storms

We all have tough days and know what it's like to experience good and bad days. We all need a place of refuge and peace where we can find protection. Proverbs 14:26 says "Reverence for the Lord gives a man deep strength. His children have a place of refuge and security." Storms are something we are supposed to go through, not live in. If you live in a storm, it will eventually tear you apart. In the storm, you need good leadership and in a family, that is the role of the father and mother.

There are three storms where you need family to help you make it through. Jesus taught us how to weather the storm and we can learn from the Scriptures how to respond in each one of these moments of life. I know there are many different kinds of storms, but here three major ones you will experience in life.

STORM OF CHANGE– We live in an era of rapid change. Any change, good or bad, causes stress. They say that moving can be as stressful as experiencing a death. Why, because it is change that will affect your entire family. The more stress you have in your life, the more stressed out you will become. What we need to know is that change is a regular part of life and therefore, we need to learn how to walk through it. Family will give you strength and courage as you go through the storms of change.

STORM OF FAILURE – We all make mistakes and will make more in the future. Failure is a whole lot easier to handle when you come home and someone hugs you and says, "We're going make it!" Fathers need to know how important it is to embrace their children when they experience failure. Father leaders know how to disciple children in their failure and help them walk through this time and learn the joy of victory.

STORM OF REJECTION–This is often the toughest one to handle. Some of the most damaging attacks occur to people when they are children. There's an old saying "Kids say the cruelest things" and unfortunately to each other. If they don't receive positive reinforcement at home through the heart of a father and mother leader then they will begin to believe what they hear from other kids. If father leaders teach their children how to handle rejection, their children will be able to face the world much stronger.

So, how does a father leader create the atmosphere of safety in the home? It's very simple but very necessary. Walk in the "four H's".

HEAR –Listen when your family hurts and do not turn a deaf ear to them. As my wife has said so many times, we need to get into their boats and one of the ways we do that is by "Listening."

HUG –Show your affection for your family with the right kind of physical contact. There is nothing quite like a hug and loving touch. A father always reaches his hand out to bless. When your son or daughter is in a storm, failure or experiencing rejection, sometimes you don't need to say anything – you just need to hold them!

HELP –Give people what they need when you are able. Families were made to help one another, not destroy one another. If we don't reach out to help as a father leader, then our daughters and sons will reach out to someone who opens their arms to them and possibly cause much more pain. How many people have left the church and families over the years because they just needed help, a hug or an ear.

HOPE–This is what we should always have in the atmosphere of the family and family of God. I have seen so many family members and church members over the years fall – beaten down by the family and by the church. Give hope by building family members up rather than tearing them down. Give hope by being the answer not the problem!

Number 2: The Family Is A Learning Center For Life

I believe we learn most of the basic life skills in a family. The Bible calls the family a garden (Ps. 144:12, That our sons may be as plants grown up in their youth; That our daughters may be as pillars, Sculptured in palace style). It's a garden for growing people. Ephesians 6:4 says we are to bring our children up with *TRAINING and INSTRUCTION* of the Lord. (emphasis added) A lot of training is simply knowing which end of the child to pat – the head or the rear. The goal is to move your child through three stages:

PARENTAL CONTROL to SELF-CONTROL to GOD CONTROL.

Luke 2:52 says: *Jesus grew intellectually [wisdom], physically [stature], spiritually [favor with God], and in social development [favor with man].* There is not much written about Joseph (the earthy father of Jesus) however, this Scripture gives us clear indication that Jesus the boy grew up in a balanced way and I believe Joseph played an important role in this. If we develop children in the areas of intellect, physical, spiritual and social, we will have brought balance to our child's life

Three things we learn from families:

RELATIONSHIPS –Right or wrong, you learned how to relate to people from your family. And many have to relearn later in life because they learned to relate in a dysfunctional way.

CHARACTER – Character is developed and is more taught than caught. Our homes need to have a learning atmosphere for life. Without character development, we will send children out without basic tools to meet society. Without the home having a teaching environment, character will not be developed.

VALUES – Psalm 145:4, "One generation makes known your faithfulness to the next." Your family relays values from one generation to the next. Values are established and not just taught. They are pillars that we live by and not just rules we obey. It's something from the inside that directs how we make decisions in life.

Number 3: The Family Is A Place To Play

God meant for the family to be a place where you let down your hair, relax and enjoy life and play. If you don't have a reputation for fun in your home, don't be surprised that when the kids get out on their own they won't want to come back home very often. If the home was a place of conflict, rules and regulations and no relationship, why would they want to come back to that environment? It's not an enjoyable place to be.

Number 4: The Family Is A Launching Pad For Ministry

Absolutely nothing unifies a family like serving the Lord together. A good example is in 1 Corinthians 16:15, *I urge you, brethren—you know the household of Stephanas, that it is the first fruits of Achaia, and that they have devoted themselves to the ministry of the saints.* Stephanas and his family were the first to become Christians in Greece and they were spending their lives helping and serving Christians everywhere. Let me challenge you to do what Joshua did in Joshua 24 when he said, *"As for me and my house, we're going to serve the Lord."*

Your Church Family

As a church family, we are to fulfill the same four purposes as the natural family. As we are a part of God's family it will make a difference in OUR LIFE and OUR SOCIETY. Every member of the church family should be heard, hugged, helped and offered hope. In both the home and the church, the "Father/Leader" is the key to making this happen. I realize we all fall short of being the leaders we should be, but let this be your goal to develop the heart of the father leader. In chapter four I go into detail about the Father Hearted Leader.

Think about these questions below and see how you measure up to the father leader.

1. What are some indications that your home and church is a shelter from storms?

2. How do I as a member of the body of Christ help those who grew up in a negative family environment?

3. What are some ways you can begin to develop the ministry in the home and church to make it truly a family with a father heart of leadership. (Both as an immediate family and a church family.

CHAPTER 4

FATHERS WITH CHARACTER & INTEGRITY

For though ye have ten thousand instructors in Christ,
*yet have ye not many **FATHERS**: for in Christ Jesus I have*
begotten you through the gospel.
1 Corinthians 4:1

This Scripture makes the statement that we have many people in our lives that can instruct us, tell us the right things to do and even be in positions of leadership, but though there are thousands of leaders, we don't have many fathers. Real fathers have character and integrity. In the next chapter I examine closer the difference between a regular leader and a father but in this chapter I would like to look at Fathers with character and integrity.

The rewards for integrity are awesome. God gives us so many promises in His word about walking in integrity and uprightness. Look at the passage of Scripture below where god promises Solomon the reward of walking with integrity.

1 Kings 9:1-9, *And it came to pass, when Solomon had finished building the house of the LORD and the king's house, and all Solomon's desire which he wanted to do, that the LORD appeared to Solomon the second time, as He had appeared to him at Gibeon. And the*

LORD said to him: "I have heard your prayer and your supplication that you have made before Me; I have consecrated this house which you have built to put My name there forever, and My eyes and My heart will be there perpetually. **Now if you walk before Me as your father David walked, in integrity of heart** *and* **in uprightness,** *to do according to all that I have commanded you, and* **if you keep My statutes** *and* **My judgments,** *then I will establish the throne of your kingdom over Israel forever, as I promised David your father, saying, 'You shall not fail to have a man on the throne of Israel.'* **But if you or your sons at all turn from following Me, and do not keep My commandments and My statutes** *which I have set before you, but go and serve other gods and worship them, then I will cut off Israel from the land which I have given them; and this house which I have consecrated for My name I will cast out of My sight. Israel will be a proverb and a byword among all peoples. And as for this house, which is everyone who passes by it will be astonished and will hiss, and say, 'Why has the LORD done thus to this land and to this house?' Then they will answer,* **'Because they forsook the LORD their God, who brought their fathers out** *of the land of Egypt, and have embraced other gods, and worshiped them and served them; therefore the Lord has brought all this calamity on them."* (emphasis added)

I believe the foundation of fatherhood is INTEGRITY! There have many books written on the importance of integrity and yet there continues to be a need to get the message out.

From this Scripture, relating to King David and his sons, I have made these observations:

- Integrity requires obedience to God.

- Integrity requires us to do what we say we will do.

- Integrity does not require perfection, but purity of heart and motive.

- God rewards fathers with integrity.

- If we turn our back on a life of integrity, there will be consequences.

Let's practically look at how we walk out integrity as a Father Leader:

Integrity in your personal life involves several areas. We call it your personal life because it is where you conduct your life apart from everyone else. It's the secret place of your life. It's where you know the truth about what really goes on. Integrity is walked out in private before it is displayed in public. It always amazes me how people think they can get by with things that everyone else gets caught in! The FATHER LEADER needs to be upright in integrity because it will affect how he leads and impacts the next generation. Spiritual and natural, fathers need to step up to a higher level of integrity. Your **personal life** will involve three areas.

Your thoughts: It's so obvious that the pornography industry is at an all time high. There are more people involved with pornography now than ever before in history. It's such a trap of destruction to character and integrity. What you practice in your thoughts will eventually become routine. It is so important that we stay pure and constantly wash our minds and hearts in the word of God. There is an old saying that is quite biblical – you are what you think! I know your thoughts will affect your job, your marriage and your family.

Your devotion: Are you growing in your faith and in your spirituality? Are you the example of how we are to be devoted to the right things of life? Do you apply your time to the right things that show your devotion to righteousness?

Your tough times: What you are made of really comes to light when you go through tough times. Your integrity is on full display when the stress of life hits you. Are you going to fall apart when you get to those places or will you display the strength of a leader to those who are watching and following you, the ones you have influence on, the sons and daughters you are impacting. You will affect them one way or another.

Integrity in your professional life is another place for Father Leaders to grow. Integrity is seen by many of our everyday actions. It's viewed by those we work with, by those we work for and by those who work for you. Since men are in the workplace so much, examine the integrity level of your professional life.

Do more than is required. Be the kind of Father Leader that goes the extra mile. Don't just do the job, do the job with excellence. Excel where you are planted and the promise is that promotion will come to you. Too many people have an 8-5 mentality and are in it for just a paycheck.

Take only what is yours. Integrity does what is right. The stories about how much is taken from the workplace every day is staggering. It's called stealing and leaders with integrity abide by the Ten Commandments and do not steal.

Help those around you reach their destiny. If you will make it your responsibility to help those around you reach their destiny, you then have taken on the role of a Father Leader in the workplace. But it's not my job.... Make it your job!

Integrity in your public life. Just as you have a private life, so you have the life that everyone sees. We have all made jokes about those in politics, or those in any form of life where you are highly visible. You have an incredible opportunity, let your integrity be on display. Two ways your integrity will shine:

Your witness in society–Because there is so many that fall short in displaying good character, honesty and loyalty; you can be an awesome witness to our society. Just a little light will be a bright light in a dark place. We need more lights of character to shine in our society. Make it your choice to be one of those lights.

Your contribution to society–Not only your witness, but your contribution to society as well. You can make a contribution that will bring lasting change that will even be known after you are gone. A positive contribution flows out of integrity, where a negative contribution flows from deception and dishonesty.

Integrity with people. The golden rule – do unto others as you would have them do unto you. There are so many ways this is seen in our life. Let me give you some bullet points on integrity with people:

- Treat others as you would have them treat you.

- Do what you say you are going to do.

- Be on time to appointments.

- Follow through when you give a commitment.

Integrity with your priorities. Always keep an eternal prospective with your priorities. That simply means your decisions need to be made with the eternal perspective at the front instead of them fitting in the back. How does this work? Always ask – does the decision I'm about to make have eternal value? Is the move across state going to be what glorifies God? Am I doing this for the right reasons or am I just making a monetary decision? How does it affect the destiny of my children? These are the kinds of questions we need to be asking on a regular basis. If we don't keep the eternal perspective, we will be making decisions that satisfy our flesh. Also, make your calendar match your priorities. If you don't take charge of your calendar, it will take charge of you and run your life. God wants your calendar to match His!

Integrity with your money. If you examine a person's checkbook, you will find very quickly where that person's heart is. Integrity in your pocketbook means you have cultivated a generous spirit. You are a giver and not a taker. I believe we should be the kind of leaders that love to give more than take. The Bible tells us it is more blessed to give than to take. We should also be a cheerful giver in God's work. As father leaders, our sons and daughters should never see us with a grudging attitude about blessing and giving to the church, people in need and missions. If you give more than you get, then you are setting an example for the next generation to follow.

Integrity in your marriage. This involves physical, emotional and spiritual leadership. As father leaders, we should demonstrate physical integrity in our marriage and with our wives. We as the leader set the standard of righteousness in our home. We are true to our vows and we are physically pure in every aspect of our lives. Emotionally, we should be strong and courageous in the walk of life. Our standard of strength should be the leadership role in the home and marriage. Spiritually, father leaders take the lead. Too many wives have been put into the position of leading the family to church. Men, this is your highest calling – to lead your family into the ways and paths of the Lord. If you do not display spiritual integrity, your children will grow up having missed one of the greatest lessons of life.

There are biblical principles for character development. If we follow the word of God and obey what it teaches us, we will reap the rewards. Examine some of these principles and the Scriptures that teach us of the rewards.

The spiritual seeds you plant in your life will bear a fruitful harvest.

Galatians 6:7, Do not be deceived, God is not mocked; for whatever a man sows, that he will also reap. What a simple yet powerful truth. What a man sows, that will he reap. When we sow good seed, the result is good harvest. Bad seeds produce bad harvest. Good character will produce that good harvest.

Your thought life determines your lifestyle. *Proverbs 23:6, Do not eat the bread of a miser, nor desire his delicacies;* As a man thinks in his heart, so is he. We know that we will become what we think and meditate on. The power of our thought life! It's the source of where our actions come from.

Don't allow the world around you to squeeze you into its mold. *Romans12:2, And do not be conformed to this world, but be transformed by the renewing of your mind, that you may prove what is that good, and acceptable, and perfect, will of God.* The mind must be renewed on a daily basis or you walk in the trap of being conformed into the worlds thinking process and mold.

Personal and spiritual growth will require concentrated and focused effort. *Philippians 4:8, Finally, brethren, whatever things are true, whatever things are noble, whatever things are just, whatever things are pure, whatever things are lovely, whatever things are of good report, if there is any virtue and if there is anything* *praiseworthy– meditate on these things.* Meditating on the things that are pure, lovely, and good is something that takes effort and diligence in a world that is filled with negativity.

The Christian father leader's life is commitment to growth, in obedience to God's Word and lived out in holiness. *Hebrews 12:1-2, Therefore we also, since we are surrounded by so great a cloud of witnesses, let us lay aside every weight, and the sin which so easily ensnares us, and let us run with endurance the race that is set before us, looking unto Jesus, the author and finisher of our faith, who for the joy that was set before Him endured the cross, despising the shame, and has sat down at the right hand of the throne of God.* If we are not committed to growth and obedience to God's word, then we will never live out our lives with integrity and character which is Holiness.

I love the Scripture in **Romans 12:9-21.** Here are great statements about integrity. Check out the practical truth entitled ***BEHAVE LIKE A CHRISTIAN.*** I would have titled it **"Live with Character and Integrity."**

Verse 9   *Let love be without hypocrisy. Abhor what is evil. Cling to what is good.*

Verse 10   *Be kindly affectionate to one another with brotherly love, in honor giving preference to one another;*

Verse 11   *not lagging in diligence, fervent in spirit, serving the Lord;*

Verse 12   *rejoicing in hope, patient in tribulation, continuing steadfastly in prayer;*

Verse 13	*distributing to the needs of the saints, given to hospitality.*
Verse 14	*Bless those who persecute you; bless and do not curse.*
Verse 15	*Rejoice with those who rejoice, and weep with those who weep.*
Verse 16	*Be of the same mind toward one another. Do not set your mind* on high things, but associate with the humble. Do not be wise in your own opinion.
Verse 17	*Repay no one evil for evil. Have regard for good things in the sight of all men.*
Verse 18	*If it is possible, as much as depends on you, live peaceably with all men.*
Verse 19	*Beloved, do not avenge yourselves, but rather give place to wrath; for it is written, "Vengeance is Mine, I will repay," says the Lord.*
Verse 20	*Therefore "If your enemy is hungry, feed him; if he is thirsty, give him a drink; for in so doing you will heap coals of fire on his head."*
Verse 21	*Do not be overcome by evil, but overcome evil with good.*

Walking in character and integrity will bring many rewards to your life. These are the kinds of rewards that will be seen as you walk them out. No instant gratification here, but lifelong rewards will be seen.

A man with integrity will **build trust in people** around

them. Cavett Roberts said: *"If my people understand me, I'll get their attention. If my people trust me, I'll get their action."* We have no idea how much influence, integrity and character will bring value to your leadership role in life. You will be a true father leader! Emerson said, *"Every great institution is the LENGETHENED shadow of a single man. His character determines the character of the organization."*

When you walk in integrity and character, you choose to walk with high standards. When you make a decision to do the right thing it says to those watching you that you are a responsible person. Our reputation is so much more valuable than our image. Image is what people think we are where integrity is what we really are. Question…. What are you really all about? What are you building? If you are building image, it will not last! Do you care more about what people think about your decisions or about what is the right decision?

I am a Twitter and follow several other tweeters (Philink is my Twitter name). On Twitter there are so many quotes about integrity. Here are some I've taken:"Integrity means you are you the same person no matter who you are with." "Integrity means you are same person when you are alone." "Integrity means living it myself before leading others." "Integrity helps a father leader be credible, not just cleaver." Billy Graham said "Integrity is the glue that holds our way of life together. We must constantly strive to keep our integrity intact. When wealth is lost, nothing is lost, when health is lost, something is lost but when character is lost, all is lost."

CHAPTER 5

THE FATHER HEARTED LEADER

FATHERS vs. REGULAR LEADERS

Fatherhood is not for the faint of heart. True fatherhood comes from the passion of wanting to see our sons and daughters grow up to become healthy, balanced, respectful adults who are able to give back to the world they have grown up in. So it is true that being a father who is making a difference in his child's life requires both art and skill– just like any craftsman will tell you.

The Art of fathering comes from the **heart** of a man. It is the passion he has for his sons. There is a naturalness that some men have in being a father, though all men are able to be nurturers and provide for the closeness and intimacy that children need.

Though we have so many teachers, leaders, role models, authority figures and even mentors, we have great need in our country, our churches and in our families for the real fathers to stand up. I will share with you the comparison between a REGULAR LEADER and a FATHER. Again, 1 Corinthians 4:15 shows us the need for fathers, "Though you have ten thousand instructors in Christ, yet you have not many fathers…" The Message Bible states it this way: *"There are a lot of people around who can't wait to tell you what you've done wrong, but there aren't many fathers willing to take the time and effort to help you grow up. It was as Jesus helped me proclaim God's Message to you that I became your father."*

Fathers have a desire to make the right choices. They have a long list of priorities they keep. They walk in great relationship with others and his family and desire to pour their lives into others. They want to see their sons and daughters become fathers and mothers as well. They understand their purpose of being a father and want to be the role model for their own children as well as other fathers.

There is a skill part to fathering as well as an art to fathering, but fathering is something you grow into more than just learn about. As your child is growing and becoming the person he or she is intended to be, you are growing and becoming the father you need to be. Make a determination to grow with your children. Make a decision that you are going to be more than a regular leader. Don't let society form you into what it says fathers should be, but be part of the new generation of fathers that have a desire to change the next generation.

In the last chapter and verse in the Old Testament, the Message Bible reads, *"He will convince parents to look after their children and children to look up to their parents. If they refuse, I'll come and put the land under a curse."* **If we have ever seen the nation under a curse, today is that day! WE NEED A FATHER REFORMATION!**

What God is saying today and from the very beginning is – Raise up and release SONS. **FATHERS** *–GATHER, EMPOWER & RELEASE.* **A father is more than a leader.** While we need leadership skills and always need to develop our leadership abilities, God intended that we be "Father Hearted Leaders."

***FATHER HEARTED LEADERS* DEMONSTRATE LOVE** by nurturing their children. They give themselves to their children and they provide for their children. First Thessalonians 2:4-8, *"Be assured that when we speak to you **we're not after crowd approval**– only God approval. Since we've been* *put through that battery of tests, you're guaranteed that both we and the Message are **free of error, mixed motives, or hidden agendas. We never used words to butter you up.** No one knows that better than you. And God knows we never used words as a smoke screen to take advantage of you. Even though we had some standing as Christ's apostles, **we never threw our weight around or tried to come across as important, with you or any-one else.** We weren't aloof with you. **We took you just as you were. We were never patronizing, never condescending, but we cared for you the way a mother cares for her children. We loved you dearly.** Not content to just pass on the Message, **we wanted to give you our hearts**. And we did." (emphasis added)*

***FATHER HEARTED LEADERS* TRAIN AND DISCI-PLINE** by directing their children. They take responsibility for their children and realize it's their responsibility to train their children. Hebrews 12:5-13, *"....Or have you forgotten **how good parents treat children,** and that God regards you as his chil-dren? **My dear child, don't shrug off God's discipline, but don't be crushed by it either. It's the child he loves that he disci-plines; the child he embraces, he also corrects. God is edu-cating you; that's why you must never drop out. He's treating you as dear children. This trouble you're in isn't punishment; it's training, the normal experience of children. Only irrespon-sible parents leave children to fend for themselves.** Would you prefer an irresponsible God? **We respect our own parents for training and not spoiling us**, so why not embrace God's training so we can truly live? **While we were children, our parents did what seemed best to them**. But God is doing what is best for us, training us to live God's holy best. At the time, discipline isn't much fun. It always feels like it's going against the grain. Later, of course, it pays off handsomely, **for it's the well-trained who find themselves mature in their relationship with God.** So don't* *sit around on your hands! No more dragging your feet!* **Clear the path for long-distance runners** *so no one will trip and fall, so no one will step in a hole and sprain an ankle. Help each other out. And run for it!"(emphasis added)*

Proverbs 22:6 says to *"Train up a child in the way he should go, And when he is old he will not depart from it."* The words ***"Train up a child"*** could be translated ***"Touch the pallet."*** What Solomon was trying to teach us here is that we as parents are responsible to *"touch the pallet"* of our children. In the old days, before the baby foods like Gerber, (you know those mashed carrots and peas that are so yummy – HA) the way the mother would feed the child when they were young was interesting. She took a spoon full of what was being served for dinner or lunch, put it in her mouth and chewed it up until it was very soft and mushy. The digestive juices in the mouth would begin the breakdown of the food so it was not so difficult for the child to eat. She would then put her finger in her mouth, get it full of the food and then put that pre-digested food into her child's mouth. They called it ***"touching the pallet of the child."*** She didn't let her neighbor, friend or even pastor touch the pallet of her child. Who would want someone else's saliva in their child's mouth? What's the lesson here? YOU, the father and mother are responsible for touching the pallet of your child. Touch the pallet of your child when they are young and when they are old, they will not depart from it. FATHER LEADERS TOUCH THE PALLET OF THEIR CHILDREN!

***FATHER HEARTED LEADERS* PROVIDE FOR THEIR CHILDREN.** That means they sustain and enrich them. You are the one who is responsible for being the provider of their needs, not their wants. The Bible tells us that a wise man even leaves an inheritance for his grandchildren. I love the term building a legacy. This means leaving something for your children that is much more valuable then silver and gold. Remember this: **PRESENTS** *are shallow while* **PRESENCE** *will help mold a life.*

FATHER HEARTED LEADERS **BLESS AND IMPART.**

Not only should the home have a teaching environment, but there should be an attitude to release your children into their destiny. I will get into this more in chapter 7 and chapter 9. If there is an atmosphere of impartation then your children will know that you desire for them to be everything God wants them to be. Proverbs 13:12 says, *"Hope deferred makes the heart sick, But when the desire comes, it is a tree of life."* Our sons and daughters need to be filled with hope for the future. Much more on blessing your children with the father's blessing in chapter 9.

FATHERS vs. REGULAR LEADERS

Many years ago, I began developing this list of comparisons between Regular Leaders and Fathers. As I saw leaders in the church and leaders in the workplace, I realized there was a major difference between a Leader and a Father. God wants us to be FATHER LEADERS – that's a great leader with a father's heart for people. In this list of comparisons, you can say **Father Pastor** vs. the **Regular Leader Pastor** or **The Father CEO** vs. the **Regular Leader CEO**. You can say the **Father Politician** vs. the **Regular Politician**.

A FATHER: Will stand with you when in difficulty.
REGULAR LEADER: *Will leave you when you have difficulty.*

A FATHER: Wants you to be a father too.
   REGULAR LEADER: Wants you to stay under him.

A FATHER: Teaches you to trust yourself.
   REGULAR LEADER: Teaches you to see him first.

A FATHER: Enjoys his son's success.
   REGULAR LEADER: Intimidated by his son's success.

A FATHER: Wants to help you with nothing in return.
   REGULAR LEADER: Wants something in return.

A FATHER: Looks for a family.
   REGULAR LEADER: Looks for a crowd.

A FATHER: Endeavors to mend the net of the family.
   REGULAR LEADER: Distracted with their own vision.

A FATHER: Will put you on his shoulders and let you see the world.
   REGULAR LEADER: Will show you the world though their eyes.

A FATHER: Asks "What can I do to help you?"
   REGULAR LEADER: Says, "Come help me" or "Go do this."

A FATHER: Wants to help you fulfill your Destiny.
   REGULAR LEADER: Wants you to help him fulfill his dream.

A FATHER: Will always walk beside you.
   REGULAR LEADER: Will always walk in front of you.

A FATHER: Is always concerned about BEING.
REGULAR LEADER: Is more concerned about DOING.

If you are in a place where you have failed as a father, don't let discouragement hold you back from making changes. THOUGH YOU CANNOT GO BACK AND MAKE A BRAND NEW START, MY FRIEND, ANYONE CAN START FROM NOW AND MAKE A BRAND NEW END.

CHAPTER 6

FATHER HEARTED CHURCHES

When you study the early church, you see the heart of the father in the leaders. Because of that, you can see the demonstration of fathering coming through Paul, Timothy, and so many of the apostles. When we follow the biblical patterns, we get biblical results. You see, God never intended for the church to be more of an organization than a family. When you read Scriptures for the family such as Ephesians 6:1-4, you see the same promise God gives to the family to the church and its leaders or rather Father Leaders.

"Children, obey your parents in the Lord, for this is right. "HONOR YOUR FATHER AND MOTHER," which is the first commandment with promise: "THAT IT MAY BE WELL WITH YOU AND YOU MAY LIVE LONG ON THE EARTH." And you, fathers, do not provoke your children to wrath, but bring them up in the training and admonition of the Lord." (emphasis added)

The Scripture that I have shared several times already, 1Corinthians 4:15, *For though you might have ten thousand instructors in Christ, yet you do not have many fathers; for in Christ Jesus I have begotten you through the gospel*...puts the emphasis on father leadership. I am concerned that we have developed a church that puts more importance on LEADERSHIP than we do on FATHERS in LEADERSHIP POSITIONS. What will this produce in the long run? I think it produces a corporate mentality in the church. It produces a machine that is not concerned about quality but quantity, performance rather than lifestyle and instant results rather than longevity. Without the FATHER LEADER model, when someone goes through a difficult time or ceases to generate output, we discard them rather than grow them through their difficult times. When someone slips and falls, restoration is not in the church mentality. We just throw them out rather than restore them to the place of value. In Galatians 6:1-3, Paul's instruction is out of the heart of a FATHER LEADER. *Brethren, if a man is overtaken in any trespass, you who are spiritual restore such a one in a spirit of gentleness, considering yourself lest you also be tempted. Bear one another's burdens, and so fulfill the law of Christ. For if anyone thinks himself to be something, when he is nothing, he deceives himself.*

Look how Paul says "If anyone thinks himself to be something, when he is nothing, he deceives himself! A LEADER with the absence of a FATHER'S HEART is just that...he thinks he is the great and almighty. He is completely deceived. Tragically, that leader will hurt and discard so many people. I hear so many stories of church staffs that have fired many of their team simply because they just weren't putting out the quota. God, give us more FATHER LEADERS IN THE CHURCH TODAY!

THINGS WE HAVE BEEN TAUGHT THAT ARE NOT TRUE...

Dynamic leadership is the key to growth! As I've stated throughout the book, I am very much for dynamic leadership however, leadership with the absence of fathering is not the key to prolonged growth. If you are just looking for numerical growth, then leadership is good. If you are looking for discipleship and spiritual growth, then dynamic leadership is NOT the key to growth.

Multiplying ministries under one roof is the key to drawing people. Again, multiplying ministries can be dangerous if your thinking and heart are not correct. What's the motive? If it's done for the purpose of growth and not empowering and releasing people into their destiny, then the LEADER will always be in a CONTROL ZONE! A FATHER LEADER multiplies with the intention of growing people and releasing them.

Soften the message – this will draw people, or be sensitive to the lost. Jesus who is the all time greatest FATHER LEADER was very honest and forthright with his leadership, yet He displayed the FATHER'S HEART and therefore people were drawn to Him. The whole "soften the message" is so anti-FATHERING. What if we just "softened the message" to our children when they were growing up? A father knows when to say no! A father knows when to discipline. He also knows how to SPEAK THE TRUTH IN LOVE for the benefit of the child.

Keep your distance from people. Wow, this is contrary to the heart of the FATHER LEADER. Fathers always walk with their sons. Fathers cry and rejoice with their sons. To distance yourself from the people God has called to lead is wrong teaching. Galatians 6:6, *Let him who is taught the word share in all good things with him who teaches.* Leadership must come from the heart of relationship. I realize there are times we need to separate, but far too many leaders are just completely separated from people. This will produce a prideful, arrogant attitude that says, "I am better than you."

WHAT I HEAR IN THE CRY OF THE CHURCH TO-DAY

We want the church to be the church we read about in the Bible. We want to follow the pattern of the Scripture – bearing one another's burdens. We want leaders that truly would lay their lives down for the sheep and will be those whose love is enough to speak the truth in love. Oh God, would you raise up true fathers in the church today!! Our patterns have produced disappointing results, so help us Lord to go back to the pattern you have given to us.

SOME THINGS I HAVE LEARNED

I have been in ministry for over thirty years and I feel like these are some of the things I have learned and observed by watching others.

- God can begin to move through your life with great leadership when leaders come to the end of themselves. True leadership is from the FAHER'S HEART, not from classroom training. Leadership skills can increase your effectiveness but will never change your heart!

- When we return to the patterns of the EARLY CHURCH, we recover the power of the EARLY CHURCH!

- The New Testament reveals that the church is God's instrument and we are very special to God! He wants us to resemble what He is all about.

- God is not looking for perfect leaders, he is looking for FATHER HEARTED leaders.

- I've learned what GOD'S FATHER HEART calls us:

A Royal Priesthood   *Revelation 1:6, 5:9-10*

A Holy Nation   *1 Peter 2:5-9*

The Body of Christ   *1 Corinthians 12:27*

God's Heritage   *1 Peter 5:3*

The Temple of God   *Ephesians 2:20-22*

The Bride of Christ   *Ephesians 5:22-23*

His Peculiar Treasure *1 Peter 2:5-9*

- God is rising up a new generation of Churches. It's a new relational church because it's built on the old relational pattern. It's an exploding church with power which is going away from the program directed church. We call it the pattern directed church. They are Apostolic/Father driven in their purpose.

- What an Apostolic/Father led church looks like. The leader's number one purpose is reaching all people for Christ and with Christ – they are completely committed to the Lordship of Jesus – have a passion for every member to be activated – have a powerful relationship with the Holy Spirit and the church.

WHAT SOME OF THE NEW TESTAMENT CHURCHES LOOKED LIKE

Most everyone has read about the seven churches in the book of Revelation. What I remember most about those churches was the things that God had against them. While a good father is ready to point out the wrong, let me remind you that they did have some good attributes as well. Look at some of the New Testament churches and what they were known for:

CHURCH OF SAMARIA in Acts 8:1-5 had awesome influence in the city. Great miracles became common in the city of Samaria even to the point where it was what everyone was talking about throughout the region. Philip was the Father Hearted leader of this church and under his leadership, they affected their society. *Apostolic/Father Hearted churches carry a burden for their cities to the extent that they give themselves to their cities and bring change to their society forever!*

CHURCH AT PHILIPPI in Acts 16:6-40, Paul and Silas were the Father Hearted leaders of this church. I love this church because it was known for its JOY, its JOY IN GIVING and it was loaded with powerful women! My dear friend Moses Vegh says "some of God's best men are women!" This was a father hearted church because its leaders were not intimidated by the women leaders God was giving them. This was also a mission hearted church that supported Paul. *Apostolic/Father hearted churches are financially committed to Apostles and their Vision!*

CHURCH AT THESSALONICA in Acts 17:1-7 &1 Thessalonians 2:2 was a father hearted church led by the father leader Paul. It was known for its ability to THRIVE when resistance came against it. *Apostolic/ Father hearted churches don't give up when under pressure. They Grow! Doesn't matter if it's political, financial or spiritual!*

CORINTHIAN CHURCH in 1&2 Corinthians has always gotten a bad rap for how carnal it was, but it became known for its order (showing that Father leaders can be very orderly) and for its holiness. Amazing how a father can see the potential in the toughest people. *Apostolic/Father Hearted churches will not be perfect, but they will be properly ordered and grow in the Holiness of God.*

CHURCH OF EPHESUS in Acts 20:29-34 was known for Growth, Order and Longevity. Fathers are always interested in the next generation, not just success in their lifetime. *Apostolic/Father Hearted churches will be structured for growth, order and longevity.*

ROMAN CHURCH in Romans 1:8-11 became the Gateway to the western world. It was a very strategic base of operation. Father leaders look beyond what they see and build for where it is going. *Apostolic/Father Hearted churches will reach beyond themselves and bear much fruit!*

THE ANTIOCH CHURCH

This church to me was one of the most progressive churches in the book of Acts. It was small but it was one of the greatest demonstrations of a FATHER HEARTED CHURCH. I love it because it did what the Jerusalem church couldn't do. In fact, if you compare the Jerusalem church to the Antioch church it would be like comparing the Professional Organized Church to a FATHER HEARTED Church.

> *Act 11:19-26, Now those who were scattered after the persecution that arose over Stephen traveled as far as Phoenicia, Cyprus, and Antioch, preaching the word to no one but the Jews only. But some of them were men from Cyprus and Cyrene, who, when they had come to Antioch, spoke to the Hellenists, preaching the Lord Jesus. And the hand of the Lord was with them, and a great number believed and turned to the Lord. Then news of*

these things came to the ears of the church in Jerusalem, and they sent out Barnabas to go as far as Antioch. When he came and had seen the grace of God, he was glad, and encouraged them all that with purpose of heart they should continue with the Lord. For he was a good man, full of the Holy Spirit and of faith. And a great many people were added to the Lord. Then Barnabas departed for Tarsus to seek Saul. And when he had found him, he brought him to Antioch. So it was that for a whole year they assembled with the church and taught a great many people. **And the disciples were <u>first called Christians</u> in Antioch.** *(emphasis added)*

The Jerusalem church was the prototypical church. Though thousands were saved and added to the church and apostles gathered and made decisions in the Jerusalem church, there was something missing. So many good teachings have even come from the Jerusalem model such as "They continued steadfastly in the *apostles' doctrine*, Jesus Christ the risen Lord. They had *fellowship* and intimacy with God through the Spirit through the *breaking of bread*, (meal around the Lord's Table transforming and forgiveness of Christ flowing in the church). They also had *prayers*, as the recognized source of all power and as a result, **They flourished for a season. But it only lasted approximately forty years.**(Read *Acts 2:42; 5:28, 42; 9:20; 15:35; 2John 9; 1 Cor. 13:14; Phil. 3:10; Matt.26:29; Mark 14:2; Acts 10:41; Acts 3:1; 6:4.)*

Antioch, on the other hand, was known as the progressive church. This church was far more than just an **ORGANIZATION!** IT WAS AN ORGANISM – A LIVING, CHANGING, GROWING, RELEASING AND EMPOWERING CHURCH. You see, one is "FROZEN IN TIME" while the other "LIVES ON." One is DESTROYED and the other SCATTERS AF-

TER ONE GENERATION while the other is MULTIPLIED ACROSS THE FACE OF THE EARTH! One created a pattern and FROZE while the other engaged in fulfilling THE GREAT COMMISSION and DEMONSTRATED the EMPOWERING and RELEASING of a generation to the known world of its time. The Antioch church had a *Philosophy of Ministry* which effected the approach they took to fulfill their purpose. Look at these thirteen positive attributes of the Antioch church.

THE UNIQUE PURPOSE OF THE ANTIOCH CHURCH:

IT WAS A <u>DISCIPLINED</u> CHURCH. The believers there were known as disciples, meaning they were disciplined learners and followed Jesus Christ.

> *Acts 11:29, Then the disciples, every man according to his ability, determined to send relief unto the brethren which dwelt in Judaea:*

IS WAS A <u>GRACE-FILLED</u> CHURCH. When Barnabus was sent to observe their faith, he encountered a strong grace upon all of them. They allowed the divine enablement of the God to rest upon them.

> *Acts 11:23, Who, when he came, and had seen the grace of God, was glad, and exhorted them all, that with purpose of heart they would cleave unto the Lord.*

IT WAS A <u>BENEVOLENT</u> CHURCH. When Jerusalem was hit by famine, Antioch responded with relief. A church with this heart has a deep concern when others are hurting.

> *Acts 11:29-30, Then the disciples, every man according to his ability, determined to send relief unto the brethren which dwelt in Judaea: Which also they did, and sent it to the elders by the hands of Barnabas and Saul.*

IT WAS A <u>CHARASMATIC</u> CHURCH. The Holy Spirit was freely moving in this church and its members were open to move out and be led by the Spirit. The leaders encouraged growing in the Spirit.

> *Acts 13:2, As they ministered to the Lord, and fasted, the Holy Ghost said, Separate me Barnabas and Saul for the work whereunto I have called them.*

IT WAS AN <u>INTEGRATED</u> CHURCH. Barnabus was a Jew and Levite. Simeon (called Niger, literally "black") was likely a black man. Lucius was from the African colony of Cyrene. Manaen was from the privileged levels of society, having childhood connections with Herod the Tetrarch. Saul was a former Jewish Pharisee who was highly educated, and who grew up in a strongly Gentile environment. Yet, all these men, who were racially and socially different, were counted among the same company of prophets and teachers. There was such a bond of unity among these men.

> *Acts 13:1, Now there were in the church that was at Antioch certain prophets and teachers; as Barnabas, and Simeon that was called Niger, and Lucius of Cyrene, and Manaen, which had been brought up with Herod the tetrarch, and Saul*

IT WAS A <u>GIFTED</u> CHURCH. There were prophets, pastors, teachers, elders, disciples, apostles and recognized ministers of every sort. They walked in full representation of the Five-Fold ministry. This is so contrary to the one man rule model which is so prevalent today.

> *Acts 13:1,   Now there were in the church that was at Antioch certain prophets and teachers; as Barnabas, and Simeon that was called Niger, and Lucius of Cyrene, and Manaen, which had been brought up with Herod the tetrarch, and Saul.*

IT WAS A <u>TEACHING</u> CHURCH. Paul and Barnabus taught in the church for a period of one whole year. They strengthened the believers in the Word of God.

> *Acts 11:26,   And when he had found him, he brought him unto Antioch. And it came to pass, that a whole year they assembled themselves with the church, and taught much people. And the disciples were called Christians first in Antioch.*

IT WAS A <u>PROPHETIC</u> CHURCH. Clearly, this church was a church staffed by the prophets. They appreciated the prophetic, they listened to the prophets, and they allowed the prophetic to come forth among them. They received the prophets that were ordained by God under the selection of Paul and Barnabus.

> *Acts 13:1, Now there were in the church that was at Antioch certainprophets and teachers; as Barnabas, and Simeon that*

IT WAS A <u>WORHIPPING</u> CHURCH. When the Christians were together at Antioch, their first activity was to minister to the Lord. The people depicted in Acts 13 appear determined to worship God, allowing the prophetic and evangelistic vision to be birthed in that experience.

Acts 13:2, As they ministered to the Lord,

IT WAS A <u>PRAYING</u> CHURCH. The people prayed and fasted till they heard from God. Their missionary activity was birthed out of a prayer meeting.

Acts 13:2 ... and fasted, the Holy Ghost said,

IT WAS A <u>STRUCTURED</u> CHURCH. They displayed the order in which the Presidency of the Holy Spirit was initiating, directing, and speaking to a people who followed and understood spiritual authority.

Acts 13:2-3, As they ministered to the Lord, and fasted, the Holy Ghost said, Separate me Barnabas and Saul for the work whereunto I have called them. And when they had fasted and prayed, and laid their hands on them, they sent them away.

IT WAS AN <u>IMPARTING</u> CHURCH. Before Paul and Barnabus were sent forth from Antioch, fasting and praying along with the laying on of hands were employed in order to impart strength to them.

Acts 13:3, And when they had fasted and prayed, and laid their hands on them, they sent them away.

IT WAS AN APOSTOLIC FATHER HEARTED CHURCH. From this single congregation of Christians came the most dynamic churches of the ancient world. The life and power of Antioch was not held in Antioch, but was constantly exported through wave after wave of Apostolic Teams who would be sent out and then return.

> *Acts 13:3, And when they had fasted and prayed, and laid their hands on them, they sent them away.*

Just as a Father Leader would do, the leadership of the Antioch church Gathered, Empowered and Released their sons and daughters.

The **Antioch Philosophy of Ministry** was simply this: Antioch grew by means of trans-local reproduction rather than by mere addition. The more they gathered, empowered and released, the stronger they became. Even though they were not all under one roof, they multiplied because many churches were started. A family grows larger with grandchildren and great grandchildren even though they cease to live in the same house. Antioch did not experience such great influence because it desired to establish greatness on a local level, but because they were obedient to send out and be poured out. The neatest thing of all was THEY WERE A MULTI-GENERATION CHURCH which did not close after one generation!

WHAT DO FATHER HEARTED CHURCHES LOOK LIKE?

The main concern is reaching all people with Christ! They have a passion to see every culture embrace Jesus. They also want to see the demonstration of power of the Holy Spirit along with the deliverance from every idol of society.

> *Ephesians 4:14, that we should no longer be children, tossed to and fro and carried about with every wind of doctrine, by the trickery of men, in the cunning craftiness of deceitful plotting,*

Completely committed to the lordship of Jesus! They desire for there to be a Clear, uncompromising message of the cross. The message is not filled with judgment but rather with compassion of the Father's Heart for hurting people.

> *Ephesians 4:15 but, speaking the truth in love, may grow up in all things into Him who is the head—Christ—*

Are completely made up of activated members! It is not a controlling church but a releasing church where all members share the ministry – not just one or two.

> *Ephesians 4:16 from whom the whole body, joined and knit together by what every joint supplies, according to the effective working by which every part does its share, causes growth of the body for the edifying of itself in love.*

They have a great relationship with the Holy Spirit! They are filled and being filled with the Holy Spirit all the time. They are a fasting and praying church. The Gifts of the Spirit are fully activated in every way.

Ephesians 5:17-21, Therefore do not be unwise, but understand what the will of the Lord is. And do not be drunk with wine, in which is dissipation; but be filled with the Spirit, speaking to one another in psalms and hymns and spiritual songs, singing and making melody in your heart to the Lord, giving thanks always for all things to God the Father in the name of our Lord Jesus Christ, submitting to one another in the fear of God.

CHAPTER 7

SHAPING THE NEXT GENERATION

In order to reinstate fathers in the lives of their children; we must undo the cultural shift of the last few decades towards radical individualism. We need a reformation in the family as well as in the church. Marriage must be re-established as a strong biblical and social institution. The value of fathering and the concept of mothers and fathers as a team called parenting needs to be awakened once again. Many practical steps can be taken in the workplace and in the church for this reformation to take place.

- The church must come back to the place where they recognize and minister to the whole family.

- Employers need to recognize the need to help employees raise healthy families instead of demanding they give themselves to corporate America. They can provide generous parental leave and experiment with more flexible work hours.

- Pastors and church leaders with a heart of a father can reclaim moral ground from the culture of divorce and non-marriage by resisting the temptation to equate "committed relationships" with marriage. It's time to take a stand.

- Marriage counselors can begin with a bias in favor of marriage, stressing the needs of the family at least as much as the needs of the client.

- The entertainment industry (by getting enough pressure from the public) can begin to shift what is popular by adding family values on the screen. I say enough with the glamorization of unwed motherhood, marital infidelity and sexual promiscuity.

- Let's put the pressure on our congressmen, representatives and every other elected official that we stand for family and life. If Christians will rise up, we can get the right people to every level of government.

Since I am dealing primarily with the aspect of "THE FATHER LEADER", I don't want to get into other issues even though they are certainly part of the whole problem! The problems are wide and deep, but if we are to progress towards a more just and humane society, we must reverse the tide that is pulling fathers apart from their families and a Church society that is not recognizing the value of fathers in the house of God. WE NEED A REFORMATION OF FATHERHOOD IN OUR NATION! **Nothing is more important for our children or for our future as a society.**

"But also look ahead: I'm sending Elijah the prophet to clear the way for the Big Day of GOD-the decisive Judgment Day! He will convince parents to look after their children and children to look up to their parents. If they refuse, I'll come and put the land under a curse." (Mal. 4:5-6 MSG)

In November of 1992, I was visiting my father and mother who were living in Budapest, Hungary. They were living with my dear friends Moses and Betty Vegh, so this was a real treat as Moses is one of my spiritual fathers. It was the last night I was there and Moses began downloading something into my life. What I share in the rest of this chapter is what he began to open to me. God was speaking thorough Moses in a powerful way that night. Moses and I were literally up all night long and then I caught my plane home when the sun came up. What I share with you in the rest of this chapter has changed our lives. I believe it the key to raising up sons and daughters.

One of the greatest Word Pictures in the Bible is found in Psalm 127:3-5:

> *Behold, children are a heritage from the LORD, The fruit of the womb is a reward.* **Like arrows in the hand** *of a warrior, So are the children of one's youth. Happy is the man who has his quiver full of them; They shall not be ashamed, But shall speak with their enemies in the gate.* (emphasis added)

Here the Psalmist talks about children "like arrows in the hand of a mighty Warrior". The emphasis on this passage is "arrows" as well as "in the hand of a warrior". This would explain why we are not seeing children raised in the level and with the emphasis of fathering. The children are not being fashioned and formed or rather, they are not "in the hand" of a FATHER LEADER.

Why did David use a word picture here instead of just stating there is a need for better fathers? This one line stands out as a display of the importance of the whole chapter. He was trying to get us to see a picture of a warrior with fashioned and formed arrows in his hand. You see, soldiers in David's time could not go to the local arrow store and purchase arrows for their quiver.

They were responsible for making their own arrows for battle. They would fashion and form them from scratch. Kind of sounds like raising children or discipling sons and daughters in the faith.

What was the process and the word picture David was thinking about? He had in mind something that was relative to shaping the next generation.

The shaft of an arrow had to be carved from hardwood and be straight. Bent arrows don't work well. Processing a "straight arrow" speaks formation and growth of character. *"Don't let anyone look down on you because you are young, but set an example for the believers in speech, in life, in love, in faith and in purity,"* Paul told Timothy in 1 Timothy 4:12 ... we also see that every other disciple of Jesus Christ learns character by instruction, example and then making right choices.

In the Native American culture, the arrowhead was carved from flint. The arrow's ability to penetrate comes from the pointed flint stone. The servant of the Lord in Isaiah declared that he had set his face like flint in the direction of God's call. The strength of the servant was his "awakened ears," which listened each morning to the words of the Lord "like one being taught." *"The Lord GOD has given me the tongue of the learned, that I should know how to speak A word in season to him who is weary. He awakens me morning by morning, He awakens my ear to hear as the learned. The Lord GOD has opened my ear; and I was not rebellious, neither did I turn away"* (Isa. 50:4-9). Strength of convictions, perseverance and discipline – strong enough to penetrate a culture opposed to God's ways – will only be forged as we teach the next generation to respond personally to the spoken and written Word of the Lord.

The feathers on the arrow were essential for direction and stability. They rotate the arrow and allow it to slice through the air. When Jesus – the pattern for discipleship – was released by His Father into public ministry, a dove descended on Him. His direction and ongoing counsel came through the ministry of the Holy Spirit. We all need the feathers of the Holy Spirit to fly straight and true to the intended target the Father has set for our lives. I want my children to walk in the counsel, wisdom and power of the Holy Spirit.

In an aimless generation, God has an intended purpose, destiny and target for their lives. There is meaning for their journey and God's method has always been for fathers to train up and prepare their sons and daughters. Arrows are not discovered; they are formed, fashioned, disciplined. They are cut from the root of iniquity, soaked in the image of Christ, pinned down for training and discipline, sanded, oiled, fired and directed. Discipleship is an intentional process that begins in our homes and churches and it takes time and devotion.

What David's picture was all about was the process his soldiers would go through to prepare an arrow. Here's more detail to that process:

The Shaping of an Arrow

The Material Used:

The arrows were made from a very hard twisted wood. The altar of the Lord was also processed out of that same wood. It was made of Acacia or Shitim Wood. The Shittah tree grew in the deserts of Sinai, and the deserts around the Dead Sea. Its nature was very rough (just as our flesh is rough) and when you look at it in raw form you couldn't imagine this wood would ever be used for anything. However, when processed properly, it was used for the rods that carried the "ark of the covenant," the altar and arrows for the warriors.

This is a great symbolization of how we are in rough form as children and as new Christians. Shaped in iniquity (twisted) yet strong when developed. Unprofitable in our original form but prepared for destiny when shaped. Get the picture? LIKE ARROWS!

> *Psalms 51:5, 6, Behold, I was brought forth in iniquity, And in sin my mother conceived me. Behold, You desire truth in the inward parts, And in the hidden part You will make me to know wisdom.*

The Process of shaping an Arrow:

It was a very complex process. It was not something you could do in a hurry. I don't like the word PROCESS because that means it's going to take time. Well, sons and daughters are a process and take time. It's also is done in stages. That means one stage must be completed before we move on to the next.

> *Isaiah 28:9, 10, "Whom will he teach knowledge? And whom will he make to understand the message? Those just weaned from milk? Those just drawn from the breasts? For precept must be upon precept, precept upon precept, Line upon line, line upon line, Here a little, there a little."*

So, here is the process of making an arrow.

CUT IT FROM THE ROOT. They would cut the wood from the tree. You must first get the wood from the twisted root in order to process it. As long as you are attached to your old roots, you will never become a straight arrow. In the roots are the iniquitous desires which make us twisted. If you don't cut the root, you will always have the fruit! So now, you have a twisted stick on its way to becoming an arrow.

> *Luke 3:8-9, Therefore bear fruits worthy of repentance, and do not begin to say to yourselves, 'We have Abraham as our father.' For I say to you that God is able to raise up children to Abraham from these stones. And even now the ax is laid to the root of the trees. Therefore every tree which does not bear good fruit is cut down and thrown into the fire. "*

SOAK IT. After cutting it from the root, they would then soak it in water. Submerge it entirely until it was soaked! You could say it was baptized into water! This would cause the wood, after time, to completely come out of its twisted state. In other words, it would naturally unwind itself. Different length of time for different branches, but eventually it would become straight. The

Bible says in *Galatians 3:27,*

> *For as many of you as were baptized into Christ have put on Christ.*

The longer you soak the more you become like Jesus. The more we become like Jesus, the straighter we become! Isn't that awesome?

> *Ephesians 5:26-27, that He might sanctify and cleanse her with the washing of water by the word, that He might present her to Himself a glorious church, not having spot or wrinkle or any such thing, but that she should be holy and without blemish.*

PIN IT. The part of the process that no flesh enjoys at all! After it was soaked and was pulled out of the water straight, they would pin it down to a board. They would make it as tight as possible. They knew that as the stick would begin to dry, its natural tendency would be to snap back into its twisted state. However, if it dried in the pinned state then all the resistance to go back to the twisted state would be gone. This is so likened to our nature. We easily revert back if we are not submitted to authority, if we are not under the father leadership of a pastor and if we do not have a father in our life.

A good Father Leader will know how and when to pin down his children. They will know when to say yes and when to say no. They will lead them into the things that are good for them and teach them the way of life. This is such an important time in the life of a child. It is also a critical time in the life of the new believer and the life of a spiritual son. Once the resistance is off the cords that have pinned it to the board, the straps can be removed. When a child stops resisting and learns authority, honor and respect, then you can proceed to the next steps.

> *1 Peter 5:6-7, Therefore humble yourselves under the mighty hand of God, that He may exalt you in due time, casting all your care upon Him, for He cares for you.*

FIRE IT, SAND IT AND OIL IT. They would then take that straight stick which had been cut from the root, soaked and pinned and put it in the fire. They would pull it out, sand it and then oil it. They would then fire it again! Pull it out, sand it and oil it over and over again until it was smooth and hard. This process perfected the hardening process so it would be able to hold up under pressure. This would take the rough edges off and allow the oil to soak into the wood in order to seal it.

Colossians 3:15, If anyone's work is burned, he will suffer loss; but he himself will be saved, yet so as through fire.

1Corinthians 1:27-29, But God has chosen the foolish things of the world to put to shame the wise, and God has chosen the weak things of the world to put to shame the things which are mighty; and the base things of the world and the things which are despised God has chosen, and the things which are not, to bring to nothing the things that are, that no flesh should glory in His presence.

Once this step was done that arrow in the making was as hard as steel. It could withstand the cares of life and it could pierce though the air like a bolt of lightning.

SHARPEN THE TIP. After the twisted stick became a straight rod, it was time to put a sharp tip on the cutting end of the arrow. They would do this by grinding the tip into a rock. Ah, get the picture? The Rock was the sharpening tool. Jesus our Rock is our sharpening tool as well. As we drive them or grind them into Jesus, they become sharp. They can pierce the air to hit the target.

Matthew 16:17-19, ... "Blessed are you, Simon Bar-Jonah, for flesh and blood has not revealed this to you, but My Father who is in heaven. And I also say to you that you are Peter, and on this rock I will build My church, and the gates of Hades shall not prevail against it. And I will give you the keys of the kingdom of heaven, and whatever you bind on earth will be bound in heaven, and whatever you loose on earth will be loosed in heaven."

DIRECT IT. It is now time to take the arrow to the practice range and do a little target shooting. You see, these soldiers could hit the mark, but they needed good arrows to do so. When they would shoot the arrows in practice, they could tell whether that arrow was straight. If it was off, they would put feathers in the tail of the arrow until it would hit the bulls eye. The feathers would be a symbol of the Holy Spirit guiding our sons and daughters as they are launched into the world to hit their target.

FIXING A BENT ARROW: Every once in a while you can get an arrow that will become bent. The process is very much the same: SOAK it, PIN it, FIRE it, OIL it, SHARPEN it, and then RE-DIRECT it. This is what father leaders do. They launch arrows that will hit the mark.

Listen to the purpose of ARROWS IN THE HAND OF A MIGHTY WARRIOR:

Psalms 127:5 gives us something that is so awesome concerning the next generation. It says, *"Happy is the man who has his quiver full of them; They shall not be ashamed, But shall speak with their enemies in the gate."* If you have your arrows in your hand, you will have contending authority with the next generation's enemy in the gate. When you engage yourself in shaping the next generation, we begin taking ground back from the enemy of that generation!

Go after those bent arrows. Begin the process with the ones in your own home. Ask God to give you sons and daughters in the Kingdom of God so you can be an active part of SHAPING THE NEXT GENERATION!

CHAPTER 8

THE PRAYING FATHER

The praying father has powerful authority in the heavenly realms over his children. Christian parents who do not regularly and fervently pray for their children are guilty of neglect in the highest order. It is considered neglect if parents do not adequately care for the temporal physical needs of their children. So why wouldn't Christian parents recognize it as neglect when they don't adequately pray for the spiritual wellbeing of their children?

A praying father has a revelation of the eternal purposes of his children. We have a very deceptive and smart enemy who will use anything to gain control of our children's minds and attention. Satan convinces us to focus our attention on the here and now, blinding us to our children's real needs. The urgency of everyday demands on our schedule will cause us to focus on everything but the most important things concerning our heritage. I believe we then focus too much on behavior modification instead of spiritual change. We then are guilty of fighting our battles in the flesh and not in the Spirit. Ephesians 6:12 says it so well: *"For our struggle is not against flesh and blood, but against the rulers, against the authorities, against the powers of this dark world and against the spiritual forces of evil in the heavenly realms."* Our real struggles are not flesh and blood struggles; they are spiritual struggles. Spiritual struggles must be fought spiritually. John Bunyan, author of *Pilgrim's Progress*, said, "You can do more than pray, after you have prayed, but you cannot do more than pray until you have prayed."

Specific Reasons Christian Parents Should Diligently Pray for Their Children

Children need our spiritual strength.

We have so many sources to help us in raising our children today, yet the real, lasting change is only possible through the power of the Holy Spirit. If your child does not come to a saving knowledge of Jesus Christ, he or she will have no power to overcome sin (Rom. 3:10-12; 8:7).

Christian foundations need to be laid in the life of your child.

Hebrews 6:1,2 are the basic stones that need to be established in their life. To avoid the iniquities, bad habits and struggles that so many adults deal with, we must teach them how to be free from the iniquity they were born into. A life transformed by Jesus Christ helps children protect against a life full of regrets.

Good foundations are established when we are young. Prayer, Bible study, the daily fight against sin and other Christian virtues developed in youth are a powerful defense against the strategies of Satan.

Praying for our children helps us focus on God's plan for their lives.

Living in today's world leads our thinking toward earthly goals for our children. Regular, fervent prayer focuses our thoughts on what is truly important. As we focus on the Lord, our goals for our children are more in line with God's goals for our children. Remember, they belong to God and he has a plan for each of their lives.

Our children are under constant attack from the world, the flesh, and the devil.

Knowing that our children are under constant attack should generate resolute prayer. Wartime brings a focus that peacetime neglects. Spiritually speaking, we are at war every single day. Letting down our guard or thinking we are safe from assault only makes our defeat more certain.

No one can pray for them like you can!

No one cares for your children more than you do. You have an intimate knowledge of your children that others do not have. Your intercession for them has more power than anybody else. Although you can have others pray for your children, it is no match for what you bring to the table in prayer. The power of a praying mother and father; no one will pray with your intensity. After all, God entrusted their care to you.

If you haven't been praying for your children, you have been deceived by Satan and are destroying the inheritance for your children. Father leaders can't afford to become apathetic in praying for their children. Your good intentions will never get the job done! Don't be guilty of indifference toward being the spiritual leader God has called you to be. Philippians 4:6-7 tells us to, *"not be anxious about anything, but in everything, by prayer and petition, with thanksgiving, present your requests to*

God. And the peace of God, which transcends all understanding, will guard your hearts and your minds in Christ Jesus." God is calling you to be passionate about praying for your children and others.

Scriptures to Pray Over Your Children

Here is a list of some Scriptures you can pray over your children:

Ephesians 1:17-19

Lord, give our children the Spirit of wisdom and revelation, and the knowledge of You. That the eyes of their hearts be enlightened that they will know the hope to which you have called them, the riches of Your glorious inheritance in the saints and His Incomparably great power for us who believe.

Ephesians 3:17-19

These children are rooted and established in love; we pray that they may have power with all the saints to grasp how wide and long and high and deep is the love of Christ towards them, and to know this love that surpasses knowledge, that they may be filled to the measure of the fullness of God.

Ephesians 5:1 and 21

Our children will be imitators of God and live a life of love. They will submit to others out of reverence to Christ.

Ephesians 6:1,2

Our children will obey their parents in the Lord. They will honor their father and mother so that it may go well with them and that they may enjoy long life on earth.

1 Timothy 4:12

No one will look down on our children because they are young, but they set an example for the believers in speech, in life, in faith and in purity.

Psalm 103:2-5

Thank you Lord that our children won't forget His benefits. You forgive all their sins and heal all their diseases. You redeem their lives form the pit, and crown them with love and compassion. You satisfy their souls with good things so that their youth is renewed like the eagles.

Psalm 1:1-3

Our children do not walk in the counsel of the ungodly or stand in the path of sinners or sit in the seat of scoffers. But their delight is in the law of the Lord and on His law they meditate day and night. They are like the trees planted by the rivers of water, which yield their fruit in season and whose leaf will not whither, and whatever they do prospers.

Psalm 119:18

Our children seek You with all their hearts; they will not stray from Your commands; they have hidden Your word in their hearts that they may not sin against you.

Psalm 91:9-16

Our children have made the Most High their dwelling place. No harm will befall them; no disaster will come near their tents. For He will give His angles charge over them to guard them in all their ways. They will carry them so that our children do not dash their foot against a stone. They will tread upon the lion and the cobra; they will trample them underfoot.

Because our children love You, You will deliver them, You will set them on high. They will call upon You and You will answer them, You will be with them in trouble, You will deliver them and honor them and with long life You will satisfy them and show them Your salvation.

Acts 1:8, 2:38

Our children will receive the gift of the Holy Spirit. They will receive power when the Holy Spirit comes upon them.

Joel 2:28

Thank you Lord that it will come to pass that You will pour out Your Spirit on our children; our sons and daughters shall prophesy, dream dreams, and see visions.

1John 4:4

Greater is He that is in our children the he that is in the world.

Isaiah 24:13-14 and 17

All our children shall be taught by the Lord and great will be their peace, their health, safety, protection and prosperity. In righteousness they will be established. Tyranny will be far from them; they will have nothing to fear.

Terror will be far removed; it will not come near them. No weapon formed against them will prosper.

Mark 4:20

The hearts of our children are like good soil, they hear the word, accept it and produce a crop....100 times that which was sown.

2 Timothy 2:22

Our children flee the evil desires of their youth and pursue righteousness, faith, love and peace, along with those who call on the Lord out of a pure heart.

Praying for your children is not something to take lightly. Your words and faith are so important when it comes to specifically praying for your children. One of the best ways we do that is by speaking the prayers and Scriptures over our children. Fathers, as the leaders in your homes, you have the responsibility to take the lead in declaring these things over your home. Years ago, someone handed me a list of targets you can pray over your children. I don't pray them all every day, but I do pray one or two of them every day and believe God to work in each of the areas of their lives. Attached is a Scripture to each of these prayer points.

I've had this in my "Family" file for many years and have used is consistently for my children and spiritual sons and daughters. I did not originate this list, so whoever developed it, thank you. It has been a blessing to me and others I've shared it with. May it bless you as well!

Salvation: Lord, let salvation spring up within my children, that they may obtain the salvation that is in Christ Jesus, with eternal glory. (Isa. 45:8, 2 Tim. 2:10)

Prayer: Let my children's lives be marked by prayerfulness, that they may learn to pray on all occasions with all kinds of prayers and requests. (Eph. 6:18)

The Word: May my children grow to find your Word more precious than gold, than much pure gold; and sweeter than honey... (Ps. 19:10)

Godly Passion: Lord, please instill in my children a soul that diligently follows after the Lord, a heart that clings passionately to you. (Ps. 63:8)

Love: That my children may learn to live a life of love, through the Spirit who dwells in them. (Eph. 5:2, Gal. 5:22)

Hope: May the God of hope grant that my children may overflow with hope and hopefulness by the power of the Holy Spirit. (Rom. 15:13)

Faith: I pray that faith will find root and grow in my children's hearts, that by faith they may gain what has been promised to them. (Luke 17:5-6, Heb. 11

Joy: May my children be filled with the joy of the Lord. (1 Thess. 1:6)

Peace: Father, let my children make every effort to do what leads to peace.(Rom. 14:19)

Grace: I pray that they may grow in the grace and knowledge of our Lord and Savior Jesus Christ. (2 Pet. 3:18)

Justice: God, help my children to love justice as you do and to act justly in all they do. (Ps. 11:7; Mic. 6:8)

Mercy: May my children always be merciful, as their Father is merciful. (Luke 6:36)

Honesty and Integrity: May integrity and honesty be their virtue and their Protection. (Ps. 25:21)

Self-control: Father, help my children not to be like many others around them, but let them be alert and self-controlled in all they do. (1 Thess. 5:6)

Perseverance: Lord, teach my children perseverance in all they do, and help them to run with perseverance the race marked out for them. (Heb. 12:1)

Faithfulness: Let love and faithfulness never leave, but bind these twin virtues around their necks and write them on the tablet of their hearts. (Prov. 3:3)

Humility: God, please cultivate in my children the ability to show true humility toward all. (Titus 3:2)

Compassion: Lord, please clothe my children with the virtue of compassion.(Col. 3:12)

Kindness: Lord, may my children always try to be kind to each other and to everyone else. (1 Thess. 5:15)

Courage: May my children always be strong and courageous in their character and in their actions. (Deut. 31:6)

Respect and Honor: Father, grant that my children may

show proper respect to everyone, as your Word commands. (1 Pet. 2:17)

Purity: Create in my children a pure heart, O God, and let their purity of heart be shown in their actions. (Ps. 51:10)

Responsibility: Grant that my children may learn responsibility, for each one should carry his own load. (Gal. 6:5)

Contentment: Father, teach my children the secret of being content in any and every situation... through him who gives them strength. (Phil. 4:12-13)

Servants heart: God, please help my children develop servants hearts, that they may serve wholeheartedly, as to the Lord, and not to men. (Eph. 6:7)

A good work ethic: Teach my children, Lord, to value work and to work hard at everything they do, as working for the Lord, not for men. (Col. 3:23)

Self-discipline: That my children may develop self-discipline, they may acquire a disciplined and prudent life, doing what is right and just and fair. (Prov. 1:3)

Gratitude: Help my children to live lives that are always filled with thankful hearts, always giving thanks to God the Father for everything. (Col. 2:7; Eph. 5:20)

Generosity: That my children may be generous and willing to share therefore laying up treasure for themselves in eternity. (1 Tim. 6:18-19)

In my **"Family"** file, I also have this prayer to release our children. Many times when I knew they were in a place of transition, decision or healing, I would pray over my children a prayer of release. My father and mother prayed something similar to this when I was six months old and very sick with only the possibility of living a few days. God healed me and released me from the assault against my life.

Again, when I was nineteen and needing direction when life was pulling on me to go the wrong way. This is your responsibility as it was my parents and mine. The result of my praying father has caused me to pursue the call on my life. Below is an example of a prayer statement you can have over your children. Again, thanks to whoever penned this prayer. It has been such a strength for my family.

Prayer to Release Our Children

Father, we release our child to you. We come against all the forces of the enemy that will keep our children from fulfilling the plan for their life. We speak in the name of Jesus that these children will rise up mighty, powerful and anointed, and they will be leaders of men and followers of You. We come against religion and tradition and those that say children are not important. We release them into their destiny and all that You have for them. We give our children to You and we say do what You want to do in them, through them and for them. We declare freedom over them and we speak blessing over them in the mighty name of Jesus.

CHAPTER 9

THE FATHERS BLESSING

The power of a blessing is so amazing. If we totally under-stood just what we can impart to our sons and daughters by pray-ing a blessing over their lives, then we would see this practice much more in those whom God has given to us to mentor and release.

Blessing is the opposite of curse. No curse ever happens without a cause, for *"Like a flying swallow, so a curse without a cause shall not alight" (Prov. 26:2)*. The absence of the blessing makes way for the curse to lay hold. In other words, the cause for curses in a person's life may be due to the failure of a father to fulfill his responsibility to bless his child.

"Death and life are in the power of the tongue, And those who love it will eat its fruit" (Prov. 18:21). Most are aware of the reality of spoken curses. Supernatural, demonic powers gain en-trance through evil, negative words spoken by one person over another. For instance, when a child hears his mother or father speak such word curses as, "You are a problem child. You are stupid. You never do anything right. I wish you had never been born," the curse has a right to align upon that child.

The power of a blessing is supernatural; it is the presence and work of the Holy Spirit, producing joy, peace, prosperity, fruitfulness; and providing health, success and protection. To be blessed is to be in God's favor and to have His face shine upon you.

Through a Bible study on the father's blessing we discover several vital principles to guide us in pronouncing this blessing.

God blessed Adam and Eve.

As soon as Adam and Eve were created, *"**God blessed them,** and God said to them, 'Be fruitful and multiply, fill the earth and subdue it; have dominion over the fish of the sea, over the birds of the air, and over every living thing that moves on the earth'"* (Gen. 1:28 emphasis added). **As a result,** Adam and Eve were fruitful, multiplied and had dominion because God spoke a blessing over them. Yes, He *spoke* a blessing.

Blessings must be spoken, for life is in the power of the tongue. **The Father's blessing** is for fruitfulness and dominion. Fruitfulness includes bearing children, but also much more. A father will do well to affirm the blessing of fruitfulness stated in

Psalm 1:3, "He shall be like a tree planted by rivers of water that brings forth its fruit in its season, whose leaf also shall not wither, and whatever she does shall prosper."

Isn't it amazing that by the simple act of faith in speaking blessings over another person, we can activate the power of God? Spoken blessings not only apply to fathers speaking blessings over their children, for everyone has the power to bless others in the name of the Lord.

God blessed Abraham.

God called Abraham and blessed him. *"Now the Lord has said to Abram: Get out of your country, From your kindred And from your father's house, To a land that I will show you. I will make you a great nation; **I will bless you** And make your name great: And you shall be a blessing. **I will bless those who bless you,** And I will curse him who curses you: And in you all the families of the earth shall be blessed"* (Gen. 12:1-3 emphasis *added).* God not only wants to bless us but to make us a blessing to others. **"And you shall be a blessing."**

God blessed Isaac.

God also blessed Abraham's son, Isaac. *"After the death of Abraham, God blessed his son, Isaac. And Isaac dwelt ay Beer LahaiRoi" (Gen. 25:11).* Beer LahaiRoimeans, "the well of the Living One who beholds me." There is a rich significance in the names of persons and places in the Bible. Here, Isaac dwelt at a place that was a place of special blessings where there was refreshing waters provided by the One who beholds him with Divine favor.

God Blessed His Son.

At the time of Jesus' baptism and inauguration into ministry, the Heavenly Father blesses His Son. *"Then Jesus, when He had been baptized, came up immediately from the water; and behold the heavens were opened to Him, and He saw the Spirit of God descending like a dove and alighting upon him. And suddenly a voice came from heaven saying, '**This is My beloved Son in whom I am well pleased**'" (Matt. 3:16-17 emphasis added).* Once again, we find the Heavenly Father speaking words of approval and blessing. Jesus was blessed with the anointing of the Holy Spirit, equipping Him for the miracle ministry and sacrificial death that lay ahead. Jesus had not yet performed a miracle nor delivered a sermon. He was blessed as a Son rather than for what he had done.

Here, too, is an example for us to follow. **Let the father lay hands on his children**, imparting the baptism in the Holy Spirit and blessing them with words of approval.

Isaac

Isaac took Rebekah as his wife, but she was barren. Isaac pleaded with the Lord for his wife and the Lord granted his petition. Rebekah conceived and became pregnant with twins. As the two sons struggled in her womb, Rebekah asked the Lord what was happening and God replied, *"Two nations are in your womb, Two peoples shall be separated from your body; One people shall be stronger than the other,* **And the older shall serve the younger***" (Gen. 25:23 emphasis added). "By faith Isaac blessed Jacob and Esau concerning things to come" (Heb. 11:20).* The blessings were prophetic. This is another characteristic of the father's blessing; it is prophetic; it speaks forth the Heavenly Father's sovereign purposes. God's sovereign purpose in election is seen in his decree that *"the older shall serve the younger."* We read in Romans, *"{For the children not yet being born, nor having done any good or evil, that the purpose of God according to election might stand, not of works but if Him who calls}, it was said to her (Rebekah), 'The older shall serve the younger,' As is it written, Jacob I have loved, but Esau I have hated" (Rom. 9:11-13).*

When Isaac realized that he was near death, he knew it was time to bestow the father's blessing upon his sons. It was the custom to bestow a favored blessing upon the first born. Esau was the first born. But to bestow the favored blessing upon Esau would have been contrary to God's revealed purpose. Obviously, Rebekah had not forgotten the words spoken to her by the Lord before the twins were born. For God had said, *"The older will serve the younger."* Therefore, Rebekah devised a plan whereby Isaac would be deceived and Jacob would receive the blessing of the first born.

Blind Isaac, mistaking Jacob for Esau, laid hands on Jacob and spoke a prophetic blessing: *Therefore may God give you of the dew of heaven, of the fatness of the earth, and plenty of grain and wine. Let peoples serve you, be master over your brethren. And let your mother's sons bow down to you. Cursed be everyone who curses you. And blessed be those who bless you! (Gen. 27:28-29)*

Again, we find the important principle of the father's blessing being prophetic. The blessing expresses the very mind and purpose of God. I believe this is extremely important. It opens up Heaven's window to Divine favor in a person's life. When Isaac discovered that he had been deceived, not having blessed the first-born as he had thought, he *"trembled exceedingly" (Gen. 27:33).* When Esau realized his brother had robbed him of the coveted blessing, he was furious and *"cried with an exceeding great and bitter cry" (Gen. 27:34).* He begged his father for a blessing for himself. Esau's desperate plea for his father's blessing reveals just how important the father's blessing is. His entire future welfare rested on this blessing. So, he said to his father, *"Have you not reserved a blessing for me? ... Have you only one blessing, my father" (Gen 27:36, 38).* Whereupon Isaac spoke the following blessings on Esau: *Behold, your dwelling shall be on the fatness of the earth, And of the dew of heaven from above. By your sword you shall live, And you shall serve your brother; And it shall come to pass, when you become restless, That you shall break his yoke from your neck (Gen. 27:39-40)*

The writer of Hebrews gives us a pertinent insight into Isaac's blessing. It was spoken in *faith!* Indeed, a prophetic blessing IS spoken in faith and received by faith. There may be no existing evidence that the spoken blessing has any substance in fact. A prophetic blessing has any substance in fact. A prophetic blessing even extends past the death of both the blesser and the blessed. Isaac's faith looked beyond death; his confident faith saw that God's purposes were not frustrated by death. He spoke with divinely imparted assurance of what would happen in the future. **A blessing given according to God's leading can-**

not fail.

By faith Isaac blessed Jacob and Esau concerning things to come. By faith Jacob, when he was dying, blessed each of the sons of Joseph, and worshipped, leaning on the top of his staff (Heb. 11:20-21).

Here is yet another principle that applies to the father's blessing – it is given in an act of worship. As Jacob blessed his sons he **"worshipped, leaning on the top of his staff" v.21.** Yes, the father's blessing is to be given in an attitude of worship. The early father is speaking on behalf of the Heavenly Father!

Jacob Blessed His Grandsons

Not only should a father bless his children, but he should also bless his grandchildren. Upon request, Jacob blessed his grandchildren, Ephraim and Manasseh and he said to Joseph, *"Please bring them to me, and I will bless them" (Gen. 48:9).* The ideal is for the children's father to request this blessing of the grandfather as Joseph did. When the ideal is not feasible, the grandfather should take the initiative to bless his grandchildren.

Joseph attempted to have the major blessing given to Manasseh, the firstborn, but Jacob crossed his hands to pick out Ephraim for the greater blessing. This demonstrates that God cannot be manipulated. He fulfills His purposes as He pleases and is not bound by human opinion or tradition. His blessing upon the two boys was prophetic, reflecting God's purpose for their lives. *"God, before whom my fathers Abraham and Isaac walked, The God who has fed me all my life long to this day, The Angel who has redeemed me from all evil, Bless the lads; Let my name be named upon them, And the name of my fathers Abraham and Isaac; And let them grow into a multitude in the midst of the earth (Gen. 48:15-16).*

Jacob Blessed His Twelve Sons

"And Jacob called his sons and said, 'Gather together, that I may tell you what shall befall you in the last days'" (Gen. 49:1). Jacob pronounced a prophetic blessing over each of his twelve sons, confirming what we have noted already, that the father's blessing is a personal, spoken prophecy foretelling future dealings of God in an individual's life. This blessing is not a generic, one-size-fits-all, but a personal prophecy as the Bible plainly states: *"And he (Jacob) blessed them; he blessed each one according to his own blessing"* (Gen. 49:28).

David Blessed His Household

It was a very special day in the life of King David. The Ark of the Covenant, which had been absent from Jerusalem for several years, is restored and placed in the tabernacle of David. There is great celebration as thirty thousand choice men of Israel escort the ark amid singing, shouting, playing of instruments and David dancing before the Lord with all of his might. After sacrifices had been offered,

David composed a special psalm and designated praisers to worship and praise God day and night before the Ark of God's presence. Then, *"He blessed the people in the name of the Lord of hosts"* and *"returned home to bless his household:* (2Sam. 6:18, 20).

Amazing! After one of the most important and physically demanding days in David's life, he was thinking about his family and was anxious to get home to bless them. Public worship did not replace the need for family ministry. Sadly, David's wife, Michal, was critical of her husband's behavior, and by rejecting her blessing she received a curse. *"Therefore Michal the daughter of Saul had no children to the day of her death"* (2 Sam. 6:23).

Another key insight into **the father's blessing** shows up in this text. Blessing is not limited to children, but should include everyone in a man's household. The father's blessings upon his wife, children, and extended family are to be continual, a daily expression of love's covering. **"Bless"** in both Hebrew and Greek means **"to declare happy."** Happy indeed is the family whose husband and father makes it his practice to speak a daily blessing over each one!

Jesus Blessed Children

One of my favorite examples: the disciples evidently thought that little children were unimportant to Jesus, and they were preventing parents from bringing them to Him, but Jesus said, *"Let the little children come to Me, and do not forbid them" (Luke 18:16). "Then little children were brought to Him that He might put his hands on them and pray" (Matt. 19:13).* The laying on of hands represents impartation. Jesus imparted blessings on little children. We will do well to follow Jesus' example.

THE PRIESTLY BLESSING

When the Levitical priesthood was established, the priests were instructed by God to bless the children of Israel. Thus, one of the duties of a priest is to bless the people. Under the New Covenant, believers become *"a royal priesthood" (1 Pet. 2:9).* So, every believer is to be a blesser of others. Here is the prescribed blessing God gave the priests:

The Lord bless you and keep you; The Lord make His face shine upon you, And be gracious to you; The Lord lift up His countenance upon you, And give you peace. (Num. 6:24-26 emphasis added)

There are two types of PROPHETIC blessings: **the personal prophetic** and the **general prophetic**! It is a blessing of good-will that imparts God's favor, protection and peace to all

God's children. It especially expresses God's desire for intimate relationship with His people. **A father's blessing can be either a personal prophesy or a positive confession and prayer for God's favor.** Even the specific elements within the general blessing can be Holy Spirit inspired and in accord with God's revealed purposes.

The father's blessing

As a father leader, it is your privilege to lay hands on your children as well as people who have never experienced such a blessing and impart a personal, prophetic blessing. People who have never been blessed by their earthly fathers are especially blessed to hear that God and their spiritual father loves them and they are special and have a special purpose in being born and brought into God's Kingdom.

Also, be an encouragement to those who need a father, who have never experienced a blessing and watch the power of a blessing release and heal them from the inside out.[xii]

(ENDNOTES)

1 David Popenoe, *Life Without Father,* (Harvard University Press, 1999).

2 Jim Daly, "The Fatherless family," (Focus on the Family; January 2006; http://www.focusonthefamily.com/about_us/profiles/jim_daly/ messages/200601-the-fatherless-family.aspx.

3 From Family Research Council; http://www.frc.org/.

4 Facts and Figures – National Statistics; http://www.afsp.org/index. cfm?fuseaction=home.viewpage&page_id=050fea9f-b064-4092-b1135c3a70de1fda.

5 *The Politics of Fatherlessness in America*, (New York: St. Martin's Press, 1998), D. Blankenhorn, *Fatherless America*, (New York: BasicBooks, 1995).

6 Rick Johnson , *The Power of a Man,* (Grand Rapids, MI: Revell Books, 2009).

7 Chambers, *Making Fathers Pay* – the wife is the moving party in divorce actions seven times out of eight. (Chicago: University of Chicago Press, 1979), 29. Hite, *Women and Love: A Cultural Revolution in Progress*, where it is stated "ninety-one percent of women who have divorced say they made the decision to divorce, not their husbands." (New York: Alfred A. Knopf, 1987), 459.

8 CHILD TRENDS DATA BANK – *childtrendsdatabank.org*

9 CHILD TRENDS DATA BANK – *childtrendsdatabank.org*

10 Weitzman, "The Divorce Revolution: The Unexpected Social and Economic Consequences for Women and Children in America," (New York:

The Free Press, 1985), 460.

11 J Kelly, Assoc. of Family and Conciliation Courts, California Chapter Mtg, Sonoma, CA, Jan. 1991.

12 Special thanks to The Children's Bread Ministries for permission to use a large portion of this text for this chapter from the booklet "The Father's Blessing" by Frank D. Hammond.

PHIL STERN

Information on how you can book Phil Stern

for a special meeting:

Link Ministries / Destiny Church

Email: philstern@linkmin.org

Connect with us on the web:

www.linkmin.org

www.destinychurch.com

www.destinychurch.org

Phone:

314-965-2122

636-734-7771

Do you need a speaker?

Do you want Phil Stern to speak to your group or event? Then contact Larry Davis at: **(623) 337-8710** or email: **ldavis@convergingzonepress.com** or use the contact form at: **www.convergingzonepress.com**.

Whether you want to purchase bulk copies of *The Father Leader* or buy another book for a friend, get it now at: **www.imprbooks.com**.

If you have a book that you would like to publish, contact Larry Davis, Publisher, at Converging Zone Press, (623) 337-8710 or email: ldavis@convergingzonepress.com or use the contact form at: www.convergingzonepress.com.